People are saying nice things about
Your Chicken is Cooked

"Who hasn't guiltily tossed out half a chicken after staring at it in the refrigerator for a week? No more! *Your Chicken is Cooked* is full of easy-to-follow recipes for leftovers that won't seem like leftovers. The book is well-suited to any skill level and the reference section is an invaluable resource to help people buy the best chicken and store it safely. *Your Chicken is Cooked* is truly a must-have for anyone who eats chicken."

– Katherine Emmenegger, Executive Chef
Great News! Discount Cookware and Cooking School

"Rotisserie chickens represent a great value. For $5, one chicken can easily feed a small family. With *Your Chicken is Cooked*, they can do even better, because now they have 125 ideas for leftovers."

– Alan Bubitz , Costco VP Deli, Food Court & Bakery
Annual rotisserie chicken sales, 18+ million

"Don't just make chicken salad with those leftovers! *Your Chicken is Cooked* provides healthy choices for soups and salads plus dozens more for quick and easy main dishes. Quotations and food facts are an enlightening and entertaining addition, and the dessert section really is to-die-for (as in Sue Grafton's Killer Cheesecake). Anyone who loves chicken will enjoy owning *Your Chicken is Cooked*."

– Linda Larsen, Busy Cooks Guide, About.com
http://busycooks.about.com

"My involvement in the food industry began in 1967, making fried chicken at a time when fat wasn't considered bad for you. I founded Boston Chicken to take advantage of a cooking technique that's actually centuries old. We're only now appreciating the health benefits of rotisserie cooking! With over 125 choices for leftovers, *Your Chicken Is Cooked* is a practical and useful addition to any kitchen, helping cooks continue the healthy choice they made by starting with rotisserie chicken."

– George A. Naddaff, Founder
Boston Chicken (known today as Boston Market)

It's so easy to pick up a rotisserie chicken from the market these days, but the basic roast chicken with standard side dishes may get a bit boring for your family. To the rescue comes, *Your Chicken Is Cooked*, with over 100 recipes using pre-cooked chicken. This recipe collection will come in handy for your chicken leftovers, as well as those holiday turkeys, since both cooked meats are interchangeable in most recipes. As an added bonus, many of the recipes are low-fat and healthy. Finally a reason for leftovers!

– Peggy Trowbridge
Home Cooking Guide, About.com
http://homecooking.about.com

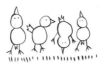

Special Thanks to You

A portion of the profits from each cookbook
sold benefits non-profit organizations
working with children and seniors.

Your Chicken is Cooked

Your Chicken is Cooked

125 Time-Saving Recipes Featuring Rotisserie Chicken

Lauren Rae Brimmer

www.YourChickenIsCooked.com

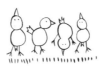

Book design by Michele DeFilippo, 1106 Design
Edited by Kate von Seeburg, K8 and Company

For information, contact the publisher, Fallbook Press
E-mail (preferred): chicken@fallbrookpress.com

First Edition

Brimmer, Lauren Rae
Your Chicken is Cooked: 125 Time-Saving Recipes
Featuring Rotisserie Chicken
ISBN: 0-9744661-2-3

Library Catalogue Information
1. Cookery (Chicken)   641.665

Nearly everyone eats chicken! This book makes a great gift or fund-raiser. Quantity discounts are available, as is customization for quantities of 100 or more.

Contact the publisher to place an order
or to discuss how we can meet your special needs.
By e-mail: chicken@fallbrookpress.com
Phone: 888.432.9984.
The order desk is always open!

Dedication

To my wonderful husband, Mark, and our daughter, Madeleine:
Thanks for inspiring me and eating chicken all the time from the
test kitchen, whether the test worked or not! xo

This book is also dedicated to anyone who makes an effort
to prepare interesting and nutritious meals at home.
You're on the right path.

Cooked Chicken Only!

This is a book about the delicious dishes you can prepare using cooked chicken meat. All references to chicken in this book mean cooked chicken unless specifically noted.

NEVER substitute raw chicken in these recipes!

If you want to start with raw chicken, however, you can roast it or sauté chicken pieces in a small amount of olive oil. De-bone, if applicable, and incorporate the cooked chicken into your chosen recipe as directed.

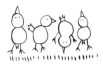

Acknowledgements

This book could not have come together without the generosity of so many. Professional chefs, authors, executives, and many of my friends and family members have pitched in.

Katherine Emmenegger – Katherine is Executive Chef at Great News! Discount Cookware and Cooking School in San Diego. Katherine is a terrific teacher and I was very honored to have her support.

Sue Grafton – I learned about award-winning mystery writer, Sue Grafton's, Killer Cheesecake (page 150) when visiting her website. Check out private eye Kinsey Milhone's latest capers at suegrafton.com

Vincent Guerithault – Owner/chef of Vincent's on Camelback in Phoenix, known for Southwestern cuisine. Thanks to Vincent for allowing the use of his Citrus Vinaigrette recipe on page 39.

George and Marti Naddaff – Both really know their chickens and have been very friendly and encouraging. Try Marti's recipe on page 42.

Jyl Steinback – Jyl enthusiastically gave her permission for the reproduction of the fat-free cheesecake recipe on page 151. Order her latest, *Jyl Steinback's Countertop Magician*, at: 866-LIVE-FIT (1-866-548-3348) or visit www.AmericasHealthiestMom.com

Special thanks also go to friends who contributed or tested recipes and gave their feedback and support to this project.

Janene Alford	Chuck and Meghan Foster
Lourie and Joe Archer	Michele Leroux Bustamante
Katherine Brimmer	Stacy Ottaviano
Keith Fisher	Jayke and Don Schrecengost

A number of people helped with the Reference section. My thanks to:

• Bessie Berry, manager of the USDA's Meat & Poultry Hotline. She and her staff reviewed the food safety sections.

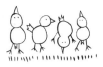

- Richard Lobb, representing the National Chicken Council and the U.S. Poultry & Egg Association. These groups kindly contributed a wealth of chicken information and recipes.

- Costco VP, Alan Bubitz, who was very helpful regarding eating trends and statistics.

- Wayne Staniec of Sentry Seasonings in Park Ridge, IL for sharing his extensive knowledge of food additives detailed in the appendix.

- The staff at LiteHouse, Inc. in Sandpoint, ID for their help with freeze-dried herbs. Visit them at www.litehousefoods.com

- Barry Koffler, on his website, www.feathersite.com, provided a variety of useful information about chicken.

- Thanks to Pam Percy for her generous contribution of material for "A Chicken in Every Pot." Pam authored *The Complete Chicken* (Voyageur Press, 2002) as well as the forthcoming, *Doris Rides Alone*, about her pet chicken, Doris. Catch up with Pam's latest at www.thecompletechicken.com

- Michele DeFilippo of 1106 Design in Phoenix has the patience of Job and a brain full of beautiful design ideas. It was wonderful having her on the team that created this book.

- Last, but certainly not least, thanks to Kate von Seeburg, a talented editor who proves the adage that no writer should edit her own work.

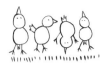

Introduction

The idea for *Your Chicken is Cooked* sprang from my efforts to eat great-tasting yet fast, nutritious meals while pregnant and working full-time.

With the increased nutritional needs of pregnancy, I couldn't skimp on dinner, even when tired after working all day. Pre-prepared rotisserie chickens paired with steamed vegetables and salad became standard fare at our house.

This book is a compilation of recipes solving the minor dilemma of what to do with the leftovers. Suddenly I had so many terrific recipes I started to buy two chickens at a time to ensure plenty of "leftovers"!

In addition to taste, I tried to be mindful of good nutrition. Personal nutrition goals include limiting trans fats (anything that says "partially hydrogenated"), saturated fats and processed foods. No one should feel deprived when they sit down for a meal, but we all need to be sensible about the quantity and quality of the foods we choose.

Keeping it simple: This is a book of simple tastes and ingredients, with plenty of tips to help you along. I may have provided more than you need, but hopefully not enough to annoy even the best of cooks.

Try to make meal preparation a fun opportunity to spend time with family! If you're single, use cooking as a chance to relax and unwind or get together with friends.

Laughter, joy, and health to you and yours! And thanks for buying the book!

> "A human being should be able to change a diaper, plan an invasion, butcher a hog, conn a ship, design a building, write a sonnet, balance accounts, build a wall, set a bone, comfort the dying, take orders, give orders, cooperate, act alone, solve equations, analyze a new problem, pitch manure, program a computer, cook a tasty meal, fight efficiently, die gallantly. Specialization is for insects."
>
> — *Robert Heinlein*
> *Time Enough for Love: The Lives of Lazarus Long*
>
> Putnam Publishing Group, 1973

Table of Contents

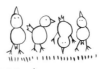

More Main Dishes

Measurements

Abbreviations included in this book:

C.	=	Cup (16 Tablespoons = 1 Cup)
lb.	=	Pound
oz.	=	Ounce
t.	=	Teaspoon
T.	=	Tablespoon (3 teaspoons = 1 Tablespoon)
Herbs		1 T. fresh = 1 t. dried* = 1 T. freeze-dried
1 Chicken	=	4 C. meat (approx. 2½ C. white and 1½ C. dark) from a 2¾ − 3 lb. cooked chicken

*As herbs age, you may need to add more to achieve the desired taste. See Recipe Notes for more information.

Terminology

mince *v.*   To cut food into very tiny pieces. Minced food is smaller than diced or chopped food.

dice *v.*   To cut food into very small (about ⅛" to ¼") cubes. Diced food is smaller than chopped food.

chop *v.*   To cut food into bite-size (or smaller) pieces. A food processor may also be used to "chop" food. Traditionally, "chop" means ¼" to ½". "Coarsely chop" means ½" to 1".

fold *v.*   Refers to gently combining one ingredient with another, generally to preserve the texture of one of the foods.

par-cook *v.*   Refers to partially cooking vegetables or other food in preparation for an additional cooking step.

whisk *v.*   Implies use of a handheld whisk. Use a hand blender or large fork if you don't have a whisk.

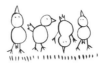

Recipe Notes

Avocados

Hass or Bacon avocados are great for the recipes you'll find in this book. By the way, the correct spelling is "Hass," not "Haas" according to the California Avocado Commission.

Both varieties should peel easily when ripe. Simply wash the avocado and halve lengthwise, (prying out the pit with a spoon) and peel. Slice or cube according to your recipe.

Hass avocados are ripe when they turn almost black and feel somewhat spongy. Bacons will remain green, but will be soft to the touch when ripe. Bacon avocados really do have a bacon flavor!

To ripen an avocado more quickly, place it in a sealed paper bag. Adding an apple in the bag will ripen the fruit even faster. For more information, visit avocado.org on the Web.

By the way, from a nutrition perspective, avocados have gotten a bad reputation because they are high in fat, but the type of fat in avocados is monounsaturated, also prevalent in olive oil. This fat, also found in macadamias, peanuts, almonds, and pecans, is important for proper brain function and has other important health benefits as well.

Butter and Oils

As Julia Child might say, in cooking there is really no substitute for butter. I try to minimize the use of butter, but I use it because I enjoy the taste. In those recipes that combine butter and flour to make a roux, you can also use olive oil or a combination of butter and oil. Try a 3:1 mix. For example, in a recipe that calls for 4 T. of butter, use 3 T. olive oil and 1 T. butter.

If worried about the impact of adding olive flavoring, look for macadamia nut oil. It's as high in monounsaturated fat as olive oil, and the flavor is a nice complement to almost any recipe.

Purchase oils that are first cold pressed and unrefined. They should be packaged in colored rather than clear containers to help retain micronutrients. Extra virgin olive oil is traditionally processed this way.

Green Onions

Also known as scallions, unless specified, remove the dark green portion and use only the white and light green parts (dice the dark green part into chives, if desired).

Guacamole

Guacamole is a healthy complement to a variety of Mexican recipes. Also serve it in wraps or atop sandwiches. Here's a simple recipe that yields about four rounded tablespoons of guacamole: Chop one large avocado and mix with a fork until smooth. Add one diced Roma tomato, 2 T. fresh salsa, and 2 t. fresh lemon juice. Some people also like to stir in 1 T. reduced-fat mayonnaise. Finish with a sprinkle of sea salt and pepper, and serve! To store for up to two days, squeeze fresh lemon or lime juice on top and cover tightly. If top gets brown (from oxidation), simply scrape off the top layer and use the remainder.

Herbs

Fresh herbs may taste best, but for maximum convenience, try freeze-dried varieties such as garlic, parsley, Italian herbs and basil. In general, 1 T. fresh or freeze-dried = 1+ t. dried. When herbs are older, you may need to add more to achieve the desired taste.

Both freeze-dried and dried herbs suffer from long or humid storage, so replace herbs bi-annually and store them in a cool dry place. Refrigerate herbs only if you live in a very humid climate. Many supermarkets now carry freeze-dried herbs, or try www.litehousefoods.com.

By the way, I learned the hard way to avoid holding freeze-dried herb containers over steaming pots when measuring herbs. Moisture from the steam is enough to reconstitute the herbs in the container.

Mushrooms

Many recipes in this book call for mushrooms, and some areas of the country have a better selection (at reasonable prices) than others. While I prefer brown mushrooms (crimini mushrooms) for their richer flavor, recipes can also be prepared with the ubiquitous white mushroom.

Sea Salt

In my opinion, sea salt is less sharp in taste than regular table salt, yet it generally substitutes 1:1 in recipes. Coarse kosher salt also seems to be gaining popularity. Since kosher salt grains are larger, their flavor absorbs more slowly, so be sure to wait a few moments and taste before adding additional salt.

Speaking of tasting, that's the only way to know you got it right, so don't be afraid to taste.

Did you know that if you over-salt a sauce or many other dishes, you can add a pinch of sugar to reduce the salt taste? Try it!

Soymilk

I've been substituting soymilk in recipes for years with great success. It has less fat than whole milk or 2% and is easier for many people to digest. When substituting soy, I recommend soy beverages (soymilk) found in the refrigerated section of supermarkets. The consistency of these products provides better results in recipes than the non-refrigerated types. For cooking, I also recommend "plain" over vanilla or other flavors.

Stock/Pan-Drippings

A supply of stock in the refrigerator or freezer will often come in handy. Making ahead saves time and allows you to skim unwanted fat which rises to the top of the container during refrigeration. Stock will keep for about three days in the refrigerator and up to four months in most freezers.

Pan drippings (the liquid that may be in the bottom of the container of pre-cooked rotisserie chicken) are extremely handy for sauces (see Side Dishes and Sauces) or simply to add moisture, so don't throw pan drippings out. Once refrigerated, this liquid takes on the consistency of jelly but will return to a liquid state when heated. Skim fat and bring to a rolling boil when reheating.

Substitutions

Recipes are about rules, and cooking is about living. Don't hesitate to get creative and create your own versions of these recipes.

Toasting Nuts (almonds, walnuts, etc.)

Toasting slivered almonds, walnuts or pine nuts is easy and fast, but it requires close attention.

In the oven: Distribute nuts on a baking sheet in a single layer. Place in the oven at 400°F for 4–5 minutes, or until lightly browned. Monitor carefully!

On the stovetop: Over medium heat, pour nuts into a pre-heated dry skillet large enough to allow nuts to form a single layer. Using a spatula, keep nuts moving constantly until lightly browned. If skillet seems too hot, simply lift it from the stove and reduce heat, replacing skillet when temperature is reduced.

Trans Fatty Acids (Trans Fats)

If a food label lists partially hydrogenated oil of any kind, it contains trans fats. Most margarines, and many prepared foods, cookies, chips, etc., contain trans fats. These are man-made, modified fat molecules that, because of their different shape, literally inhibit normal function in many areas of the body, including the brain. Many studies have shown trans fats to be worse than saturated fats.

You won't run into much trans fat choosing ingredients for these recipes, but make sure oil, chips and prepared soups don't list them. While you're reading labels, choose prepared marinara sauce without high fructose corn syrup, another modern-day food item you're better off avoiding. Among national brands, many (if not all) Barilla® and Hunt's® sauces meet this requirement.

Yogurt/yoghurt (as a substitute for cream)

I was a skeptic, but while writing this book, I decided to try substituting plain yogurt in order to reduce the fat content of recipes such as quiche. Now I'm a convert. No, it doesn't taste the same, but it tastes great. Quiche turns out light and fluffy. Salad dressing and dips get a fresh tasting zing.

The folks at Stonyfield Farm® (who make the terrific whole milk yogurts that were used in the test kitchen) recommend adding starch when substituting yogurt in cooked sauces to prevent curdling. 1 T. flour added to 1 C. yogurt is the suggested ratio. Stir in flour prior to heating.

Note that whole milk yogurt has considerably less fat than even low-fat sour cream. When comparing at home, make sure serving sizes are comparable before comparing fat grams.

Soups

Chicken Stock

Refer to this page when your recipe calls for chicken stock.

In a stockpot, place chicken carcass (with remaining meat still attached but skin mostly removed) and cover with water (6–7 cups). Include any available chicken broth from the rotisserie chicken container (*Hint:* swirl water in the container and add to stockpot to get every bit). Simmer 1½ hours or until meat falls away from bones easily and carcass begins to disintegrate. The more dark meat (and bones of dark meat) you used, the more flavorful the stock will be.

Optional ingredients: Any combination of carrots, bay leaves, whole onion or celery stalk will add nice flavor. I generally make stock with none of these additions, preferring to season as I use the stock.

Remove from heat. Strain out and discard all bones, skin, and any optional ingredients, leaving just the stock and meat. Add salt and pepper, to taste, if desired (or wait until you use the stock).

Use immediately or cool as quickly as possible, diluting with 1 C. cold water (optional to aid cooling). Refrigerate for up to three days. Skim fat from top prior to use. I leave about 20% of fat for flavoring. When you want a clear stock, skim more fat.

Stock may also be frozen. Use freezer bags to conserve space and label with preparation date. If freezing, remember to leave room in containers for expansion, and cool stock prior to placing in bags.

For best flavor and nutritional value, freeze for no more than three months. Defrost overnight in the refrigerator. **Use within 48 hours of defrosting.**

Really fast stock: Simply cover the carcass with water as above and bring to a rolling boil for 10 minutes. Remove from heat. Strain out and discard all bones, skin, etc. leaving just the stock (and meat, if desired). Add salt and pepper, to taste.

This fast stock won't be as flavorful as the slow-cooked stock above, but it tastes better than canned broth, it costs almost nothing, it's almost certainly better for you, and there are no cans to recycle or throw out.

Italian Chicken Soup with Orzo

Here's what to do with leftovers! This hearty and flavorful soup makes a great meal when paired with a fresh green salad, and it can be ready to eat in about 30 minutes (assuming available stock). Any small pasta may be substituted for the orzo (orzo is small pasta similar in appearance to rice). Serves 4–5.

In a 4-quart or larger saucepan, heat stock to simmering. Add vegetables and seasonings, to taste. Simmer 10 minutes. Add pasta and chicken.

Simmer at least 15 minutes to cook pasta and vegetables. Reduce heat and simmer gently until ready to serve. Taste and season again, if necessary, just prior to serving.

▶ *Cooking tip: If making ahead, add pasta 15 minutes prior to serving time so that it doesn't become mushy from over-cooking.*

Variation: ½ C. asparagus. Add trimmed, bite size pieces after pasta. Fresh, frozen or leftover asparagus work well. Do not use canned!

5–6 C. chicken stock (see page 14)

1 medium white onion, chopped (1 C.)

1 medium zucchini, chopped (¾ C.)

1 C. brown mushrooms, chopped or thin sliced

1 can (14 oz.) crushed Italian style stewed tomatoes or chunky tomato sauce

Italian seasoning to taste (basil, thyme, oregano, etc.)

¼ t. sea salt, to taste (adjust if stock is already salted)

½ t. black pepper, to taste

4–5 oz. (uncooked) orzo or other small pasta

1 C. cooked chicken (use up to 2 C. when soup is a main course)

A first-rate soup is more creative than a second-rate painting.

– Abraham Maslow

Source: quotationspage.com

Quick and Easy Chicken Soup

When you need a fast first course, or you're making chicken soup for a sick friend, this is a great choice. Chicken soup's curative effect on respiratory ailments was described as early as 200 B.C., and scientists now acknowledge that chicken soup (made with real stock and vegetables, not canned broth) does have beneficial medicinal qualities. Mild yet satisfying, this soup packs lots of flavor but isn't overly filling. Serves 4.

---

1 T. extra virgin olive oil

½ C. green onions, finely chopped

¾ C. brown mushrooms, chopped or thin sliced

½ C. red bell pepper, diced

5 C. chicken stock (see page 14)

2 T. fresh basil, chopped

¼ t. sea salt, to taste (adjust if stock is already salted)

½ C. chunky pasta sauce, or 1 fresh tomato, chopped

½ C. cooked chicken

¾ C. baby spinach or frozen spinach, chopped

In 4-quart or larger saucepan over medium heat, sauté green onions, mushrooms and bell pepper until soft, 3–4 minutes. Add stock and increase heat, stirring occasionally, until simmering.

Add remaining ingredients and season, to taste.

Simmer an additional 15–20 minutes. Serve and enjoy!

> Soup is a lot like a family. Each ingredient enhances the others; each batch has its own characteristics; and it needs time to simmer to reach full flavor.
>
> *– Marge Kennedy*
>
> 100 Things You Can Do to Keep Your Family Together (1994)

Chicken Chili

I adapted this chicken chili recipe from a beef chili recipe I've made for many years. Serve with cornbread (see page 136) and salad for a hearty meal that's lower in fat and cholesterol than traditional beef chili. Serves 6.

In a slow cooker or 4-quart or larger saucepan, combine all ingredients. If desired, first sauté onion in 1 T. olive oil. Simmer at least three hours (covered) if using a slow cooker or at least 2 hours on stove top. The longer it cooks, the better (and hotter) it tastes! Stir occasionally.

Serve with a liberal garnish of cheddar cheese.

▶ *Cooking Tip: If you're in a hurry, stir every 20–30 minutes, skimming water (from the tomatoes) off the top prior to each stir to help chili cook down. Reduces cooking time by half!*

> Je vis de bonne soupe, et non de beau langage. (I live on good soup, not on fine words).
>
> – *Molière [Jean Baptiste Poquelin]*
> *(1622–1673), French comic playwright.*
> *The Learned Ladies (Les Femmes Savantes), act 2, sc. 7. (1672).*
>
> Source: bartleby.com

1 large white or red onion, diced

2 cans (14 oz.) Mexican style diced stewed tomatoes

2 cans (14 oz.) diced stewed tomatoes (plain)

1 can (14 oz.) white kidney beans, drained

1 T. Worcestershire sauce

¼ C. cayenne red pepper sauce, to taste

3 C. cooked chicken, cut to small pieces or shredded

Sea salt and freshly ground black pepper to taste

1 C. sharp cheddar cheese to garnish

Tortellini Chicken Soup (Meat optional)

Tortellini Chicken Soup is the perfect choice for those days when soup will be the entire meal. This soup goes from refrigerator to table in about 20 minutes, and you'll have time to set the table and enjoy a glass of wine while it cooks! For best results, use fresh or frozen tortellini. If tortellini is frozen, do not defrost. Simply add extra cooking time and taste prior to serving. So delicious! Serves 4–6.

---

1 T. olive oil

¾ C. green onion, chopped

2 cloves garlic, minced

¾ C. red bell pepper, diced

6 C. chicken stock (see page 14)

1¼ C. chopped Roma tomatoes

Sea salt and ground black pepper, to taste

1 (9-oz.) package cheese tortellini (small)

2 C. fresh baby spinach (2–3 oz.) stems removed

1 C. cooked chicken, cut to bite size or shredded

½ C. freshly shredded Asiago or Parmesan to garnish

In a large soup pot, heat olive oil over medium heat. Sauté green onion and red bell pepper with garlic, about 5 minutes, or until vegetables are soft. Add chicken stock, tomatoes, and seasonings, increasing heat to high to bring to a boil. For a smoother texture, purée soup slightly with a hand blender.

About 10 minutes prior to serving, add the tortellini, reduce heat, and simmer according to package directions. When tortellini is almost done, add spinach and chicken. Taste, and add additional ground pepper and salt if needed.

Serve immediately. Garnish with a liberal sprinkling of cheese.

▶ *Cooking Tip: Use the smallest available tortellini and take care not to overcook it. Like most pasta, tortellini is best served al dente.*

▶ *Safety Tip: Blades of the hand blender must be well submerged to avoid splashing hot soup. Be careful!*

Potato Leek Soup (Meatless)

This elegant soup is a great first course to a wide variety of main dishes. Be sure to slice the leeks lengthwise and rinse well to remove dirt. Use only the white and light green portions of both the leeks and green onions. Serves 4.

In 3½-quart or larger saucepan, combine stock with potatoes and leeks. Use only the white and lightest green portions of the leeks and onions.

If using Idaho or other thicker-skinned potatoes, peel prior to cutting into cubes. Simmer 35 minutes or until potatoes are tender (test with a fork). With a hand blender (you can do this right in the pan) or in a conventional blender, purée the vegetables into the stock.

Add sea salt and pepper to taste, and serve!

Variation: No, it doesn't involve rotisserie chicken, but a great variation on this soup is perfect for St. Patrick's Day as a first course to corned beef and cabbage. Simply make the recipe as above, substituting corned beef stock for chicken stock and adding ¾ C. coarsely chopped cabbage (also from the corned beef stock pot). Purée, and serve as above. Delicious!

▶ *Safety Tip: Blades of the hand blender must be well submerged to avoid splashing hot soup. Be careful!*

6 C. chicken stock (see page 14)

4 large white or Yukon Gold potatoes, skins on and cubed (¾")

3 medium leeks, coarsely chopped (or 2 large)

½ C. green onions, chopped (cut tops into chives for garnish)

¼ t. sea salt, to taste

½ t. ground white pepper, to taste

Optional: Low-fat sour cream and/or diced chives to garnish

Tomato Leek Soup (Meatless)

So easy! Fresh tomatoes give this soup a fabulous garden-fresh taste. As in potato leek soup, be sure to slice the leeks lengthwise and run them under water to clean. My preference is to purée this soup slightly, leaving plenty of vegetable chunks. Serves 4.

---

6 C. chicken stock (see page 14)

3 medium leeks, chopped (or 2 large)

½ C. green onions, chopped

3–4 large fresh tomatoes, chopped (3 C.)

Sea salt and black pepper, to taste

Juice of ½ lemon

1 T. fresh basil, chopped (or 1 t. dried)

In 3½ quart or larger saucepan, combine stock with onions and leeks. Use only the white and lightest green portions of the leeks and onions.

Simmer 10 minutes, and add tomatoes.

Add sea salt, pepper and lemon, to taste. Purée slightly or simply leave the soup chunky. Simmer another 5 minutes and serve!

Variation: Try adding 1 C. of baby spinach along with tomatoes.

> Lloyd: What's the soup du jour?
>
> Waiter: It's the soup of the day.
>
> Lloyd: Mmm, that does sound good.
>
> *– Dumb and Dumber*
>
> Source: quotegeek.com

Kale Soup (Meatless)

Kale is an "in" vegetable, because it's one of the healthiest foods in the world. Very high in Vitamins A and K, iron, lutein, beta carotene, and calcium, kale tastes like a richer, sweeter cabbage. If you have extra, try the Kale and Mushrooms side dish on page 137. Serves 4.

Preheat olive oil over medium heat. Sauté the garlic, celery and carrot seasoned with salt and pepper, 3–5 minutes. Add stock and kale*, increasing heat to HIGH until simmering. Reduce heat and continue to simmer 30–35 minutes or until kale is tender (taste).

Taste and add sea salt and pepper, if needed. Serve and enjoy!

*Many grocers offer kale in bags, pre-washed and trimmed

Variation: Cream of Kale Soup (Meatless). Follow directions above. When kale is fully cooked, remove approximately ½ C. of broth to a small bowl to cool slightly. With a fork or whisk, stir in 3 T. cornstarch and blend until smooth. Return cornstarch mixture to stockpot and also add ¾ C. evaporated milk. Stir frequently, 3–5 minutes, to thicken. Serve steaming hot.

1 T. olive oil

2 cloves garlic (1 t. freeze-dried)

¾ C. celery, diced (3 medium stalks)

½ C. baby carrot, diced (8–9)

5 C. chicken stock (see page 14)

3 C. kale, washed and chopped, hard stems removed

Sea salt and black pepper, to taste

An idealist is one who, on noticing that a rose smells better than a cabbage, concludes that it will also make better soup.

— *H.L. (Henry Lewis) Mencken (1880–1956)*

Source: bartleby.com

Yummy Chicken Barley Soup with Leeks

This hearty soup is made primarily with frozen vegetables for easy preparation. Be sure to slice the leeks lengthwise and rinse well to remove dirt. Use only the white and light green portions. Serves 4.

6 C. chicken stock (see page 14)

2 medium leeks, chopped

¾ C. yellow onion, chopped

½ C. baby carrots, slivered

½ C. frozen petite peas

½ C. frozen white corn

¾ C. barley (or barley and lentil dry soup mix)

1½ C. cooked chicken

¾ t. dried thyme

1 t. dried parsley

Sea salt and ground black pepper, to taste

Optional: Low-fat sour cream to garnish

Over high heat in a large saucepan or stockpot, combine chicken stock and vegetables, using only the white and lightest green portions of the leeks.

Add barley, chicken meat, and seasonings. Taste, and adjust seasonings as needed.

Cover, bringing soup to a simmer. Reduce heat to maintain simmer, approximately 45 minutes, stirring occasionally. Taste to ensure barley is very tender, and re-season if necessary.

Top individual servings with a garnish of sour cream and enjoy!

Archaeopteryx is believed to be the predecessor of modern birds, including the chicken. A carnivore that roamed the earth along with dinosaurs, Archaeopteryx had wings and feathers, but may or may not have been capable of flight.

Potato Chicken Soup with Bacon

Incredibly hearty, this soup is reminiscent of a steaming hot baked potato. Serve with a salad for a complete meal. Feel free to add a dollop of low-fat sour cream when serving. Serves 4.

Preheat olive oil in a 4-quart pan over medium heat. Sauté the onion and celery seasoned with salt and pepper until soft, 3–5 minutes. Add stock and potatoes, increasing heat to high until simmering. Reduce heat and simmer 35 minutes or until potatoes are tender (test with a fork).

With an electric hand mixer (you can do this right in the saucepan), purée the potatoes and onions into the stock.

▶ *Safety Tip: Blades of the hand blender must be well submerged to avoid splashing hot soup. Be careful!*

Add chicken and bacon plus additional sea salt and pepper to taste. Continue to cook over medium heat until chicken is hot.

To serve: Top each bowl with fresh chives and a dollop of sour cream.

*White or Yukon Gold potatoes are preferable. If using Idaho or other thicker-skin potatoes, peel prior to cutting into cubes.

2 T. olive oil

1 small white onion, chopped (approx. ¾ C.)

2 medium stalks celery, chopped (approx. ½ C.)

Sea salt and ground black pepper, to taste

6 C. chicken stock (see page 14)

5 large potatoes, skins on and cubed (less than 1")*

6 strips of crisp bacon, drained and crumbled

2 C. cooked chicken, in chunks or shredded

Low-fat sour cream and chives to garnish

> I want my food dead. Not sick, not dying, dead.
>
> — *Oscar Wilde*
>
> Source: quotegeek.com

Spinach and Tofu Soup (Meatless)

If cooking with tofu doesn't appeal to you, simply delete it and you'll have a great soup with a little less protein. In the test kitchen, using frozen onion and fresh baby spinach (pre-washed and bagged), this soup went from refrigerator to serving in under 10 minutes, and it was superb! Serves 3.

4 C. chicken stock (see page 14)

1 C. white onions, chopped (fresh or frozen)

1 t. freeze-dried garlic (or 2 cloves, minced)

1 C. fresh or frozen baby spinach

6 oz. firm tofu, cubed

1 T. freeze-dried or fresh parsley (1 t. dried)

Sea salt and ground black pepper, to taste

Heat chicken stock in a large saucepan over high heat. When stock comes to a boil, add onion and garlic, reducing heat to simmer 3 minutes.

Add spinach, tofu and parsley, and simmer gently an additional 2–3 minutes. Taste, and adjust seasonings, if necessary.

Serve steaming hot.

> More die in the United States of too much food than of too little.
>
> — *John Kenneth Galbraith*
>
> Source: quotationspage.com

Cream of Potato Chicken Soup

This is our toddler's favorite soup. Subtle yet hearty, it's great for a rainy day. I prefer to lightly purée this soup, leaving a few pieces of chicken and potatoes to add texture and interest. Serves 4.

In a 4-quart saucepan or chef's pan, boil potatoes and onions in stock. If using Idaho or other thicker-skin potatoes, peel prior to cubing. Simmer 35 minutes or until potatoes are fork tender.

Add chicken, seasonings and evaporated milk (or wait until after the purée step to add chicken, leaving larger pieces). Purée the potatoes and onions into the stock using a hand mixer or blender. Cover and reduce heat to low until ready to serve. Delicious!

6 C. chicken stock (see page 14)

4 large white potatoes, skins on and cut to cubes (less than 1")

½ C. green onions, chopped

Sea salt and ground black pepper, to taste

¼ C. evaporated (not condensed) milk (preferably low-fat)

1 C. cooked chicken

> ▶ *Safety Tip: Blades of the hand blender must be well submerged to avoid splashing hot soup. Be careful!*

The "wishbone" custom of two people pulling on the clavicle of a chicken in hopes of getting the larger piece, and thus a wish, originated with the Etruscans, inhabitants of the Italian peninsula in the sixth century B.C.

Source: The Complete Chicken. Pam Percy. Voyageur Press 2002

Chicken Soup with Brown Rice and Mushrooms

Brown mushrooms add unforgettable flavor to this hearty, flavorful soup that's also a snap to prepare. Try it with a variety of dishes or on its own as a light supper. Serves 4 as a starter, 2–3 as a main course.

5 C. chicken stock (see page 14)

Sea salt and black pepper, to taste

½ C. green onion, finely chopped

1½ C. brown mushrooms, chopped

1 T. fresh basil, to taste (1 t. dried)

1–2 C. cooked chicken

½ C. brown or basmati rice (or try wild rice)

In a stockpot, combine stock with other ingredients, adding rice last. Cover and bring to a boil over high heat, then reduce heat to maintain a simmer.

Simmer 20–30 minutes, stirring occasionally, until rice is very tender. Reduce heat and keep warm until ready to serve.

Variation: ½ C. asparagus. Add trimmed, bite size pieces 3–5 minutes prior to serving. Fresh, frozen or leftovers work well. Do not use canned!

Tips for reheating chicken in the microwave:

For best taste, try cutting the chicken into individual servings for reheating. Leave skin on to keep it moist, but remove skin prior to eating.

Cover chicken with a paper towel to keep your microwave clean and help chicken retain moisture. Moistening the paper towel also helps. Be careful not to overheat, as meat will lose flavor and texture.

Microwaves vary, but start with 1 minute on HIGH to reheat a large individual serving (with bones) from the refrigerator.

Modern Cream of Chicken and Mushroom Soup

Flavorful brown mushrooms bring old-fashioned cream of chicken soup deliciously into the modern world. This is a great "leftovers" soup because it requires little meat to taste great. Adding sour cream or yogurt adds a whole new dimension. Leftover soup can be used to make the Chicken, Mushroom and Rice casserole on page 108. Serves 4.

In a stockpot, heat olive oil and butter over medium heat. Sauté onion and garlic 2–3 minutes until onion softens.

Blend in flour (sprinkle lightly on top of onion) plus ¼ C. chicken stock. Add mushrooms and continue to sauté 4–5 minutes before gradually adding remaining stock. Increase heat and bring to a simmer, stirring frequently.

Stir in milk and add chicken plus Dijon mustard, sea salt and pepper, to taste. Return stock to a slow simmer for an additional 5–7 minutes until thoroughly heated and thickened to desired consistency. Add yogurt* or sour cream gradually, and taste until it's just right. Serve and enjoy!

*Stir in 2 t. flour to help prevent curdling. See page 12 for more details.

3 T. extra virgin olive oil and 1 T. butter

½ C. white onion, finely chopped

2 cloves garlic, minced

¼ C. flour, all-purpose

4 C. chicken stock (see page 14)

2 C. brown mushrooms, thinly sliced (approx. 6 oz.)

¾ C. evaporated milk (preferably low-fat)

½–1 C. cooked chicken, bite size

½ T. Dijon mustard

Sea salt, to taste

Ground black pepper to taste

¾ C. reduced-fat sour cream or low-fat yogurt

An early poultry census, taken in 1880, determined that there were 102 million chickens in the United States. With the poultry industry flourishing, Cornell University was the first to offer a course in poultry husbandry in 1891.

Pea Soup with Chicken and Artichoke Hearts

This versatile 20-minute soup is a great first course to a light supper entrée, or it can be the entire meal. Serve it with crusty rosemary bread or rolls. The bay leaf, artichoke hearts and yogurt lend subtle flavors that transform ordinary pea soup into an elegant treat. Makes 4–5 servings.

---

1 T. extra virgin olive oil

2 large cloves garlic, minced

¾ C. white or sweet onion, chopped

1 large celery stalk, chopped

Sprinkle of sea salt and ground black pepper

1 bag frozen petite peas, 16 oz.

6 oz. frozen artichoke hearts*

3 bay leaves

5 C. chicken stock (see page 14)

1 C. cooked chicken, shredded (optional)

¾ C. plain yogurt (preferably whole milk yogurt

Reduced fat sour cream to garnish, if desired

In a soup pot over medium heat, pre-heat olive oil and sauté garlic, onion, and celery for 3–4 minutes until softened. Add frozen peas reserving a few as garnish, if desired. Also add artichoke hearts, bay leaves and chicken stock, increasing heat to high until soup comes to a boil. Once boiling, reduce heat to maintain a simmer, and cook for 10 minutes. Remove and discard bay leaves. Add chicken.

With a hand blender, being careful to keep blade fully immersed to avoid splashing hot liquid, purée to desired consistency.

Gently stir in yogurt and additional salt and pepper, if desired. Serve hot with a garnish of peas or low-fat sour cream.

Delicious!

► *Cooking Tip: Unsalted stock will require a significant amount of salt (probably at least 1 teaspoon). Keep tasting and add salt gradually to reach the correct level.*

*The test kitchen used Trader Joe's® frozen artichoke hearts

My Favorite Chicken Lentil Soup

This nutritious, hearty and delicious soup is packed with good things, including wonderful flavor. Lentils are a source of protein that contrary to prior belief, don't need to be combined with other protein sources (such as pasta) to be complete. Your body takes care of that requirement by providing the missing enzymes during digestion. Serves 4–5.

In a stockpot, pre-heat olive oil and sauté the onion, celery, garlic and bay leaves until soft, approximately 5 minutes. Add chicken stock and simmer 10 minutes. Remove and discard bay leaves.

Meanwhile, prepare lentils for cooking by placing them in a bowl and covering them with cool water. Discard anything that floats to the top. Drain, rinse again and add to stockpot.

Season with rosemary and cilantro. Add tomato paste and simmer approximately 45 minutes, or until lentils are soft but not mushy. Add additional stock or water if soup cooks down too much.

Add chicken and remaining seasonings.

Serve with dark peasant bread or crusty sourdough and enjoy!

Variation: To make this soup the entire meal, add a few ounces of small pasta 10–12 minutes prior to serving.

► *Cooking Tip: Unlike dried beans, lentils don't need to be soaked prior to cooking. Simply place them in water and discard anything that floats to the top. Rinse, drain again and they're ready for use. Avoid cooking lentils too long as they will become mushy. Brown and green lentils are some of the most forgiving. Orange lentils cook faster.*

3 T. extra virgin olive oil

½ C. white onion, minced

¾ C. celery, minced

2 cloves garlic, minced

4 bay leaves

5 C. chicken stock (more to thin, if necessary; see page 14)

8 oz. brown or green lentils

½ t. rosemary, dried

½ t. cilantro, dried (or parsley for a milder taste)

4–5 oz. tomato paste

1–1½ C. cooked chicken

Sea salt and ground black pepper, to taste

Southwestern Pinto Bean Soup

Using readily-available prepared ingredients, this tastes like an all-day soup but doesn't even take an hour. Searching the Internet and my mother-in-law's cookbook library, I found five white bean soup recipes for ideas, then went to the test kitchen to include some ideas of my own (such as using Pinto beans instead of white beans). Try it! You'll discover a delicious, hearty and nutritious soup with a Southwestern flair. And don't forget the corn-bread (page 136)! Serves 3–4.

2½ C. chicken stock (see page 14)

1 C. fresh salsa

1 C. white corn

1 can (15 oz.) pinto beans, drained (or white beans)

½ t. ground cumin

1 small can (4 oz.) mild green chilies, diced

2 C. cooked chicken, cut to bite size

Sour cream to garnish (1–2 T. per bowl)

In a 4-quart or larger chef's pan or small stockpot over medium-high heat, combine all ingredients, except sour cream. Use a fresh salsa with lots of chunky tomato, onion and cilantro. Corn may be fresh, frozen, or canned.

Simmer, loosely covered, 45–50 minutes. Spoon into serving bowls and serve with a dollop of sour cream.

▶ *Cooking Tip: If using dried pinto beans, they'll need to soak overnight. Place 1 C. beans in a bowl with enough water to cover. Drain the beans (discard water), rinse and use in place of canned beans.*

> Whistler: Y'know, raiding an Englishman's fridge is like dating a nun. You're never going to get the good stuff.
>
> — *Buffy the Vampire Slayer*
>
> Source: quotegeek.com

Salads, Brunch and Lunch Fare

Fruity and Fresh Green Salad with Chicken and Nuts

This fresh tasting salad makes an excellent lunch for a small group. Raisins and nuts add interesting taste and texture that complements either dressing choice. White or dark chicken meat may be used, but white meat is preferable. Serves 4.

½ C. toasted walnut halves or pine nuts

6–8 C. crisp romaine lettuce

2 C. cooked chicken meat, chopped or cubed (preferably white meat)

1 medium Gala, Fuji or Pink Lady apple, cored and cubed

1 C. red seedless grapes, halved lengthwise

½ C. raw broccoli chopped into small pieces

½ C. golden raisins

½ C. prepared Vidalia onion salad dressing*

Toast nuts slowly (no more than medium heat) in a dry skillet or toaster oven. Remove from heat source immediately when edges begin to brown, and set aside to cool.

In a large bowl, combine and toss lettuce, chicken, apple, grapes, broccoli and raisins. Chill until ready to serve.

Just prior to serving, add dressing and toss. Top with toasted nuts. Serve in chilled salad bowls.

▶ Cooking Tip: If more than a few minutes will elapse between salad preparation and serving, the apple will become brown. Either wait to cube the apple just prior to serving or squeeze fresh lemon or lime juice over the apple prior to adding it to the salad. The citric acid in the juice acts as a preservative.

*Also try prepared sweet poppy seed dressing or the oriental dressings shown on pages 42 or 62.

Two Chicken Salads
(2 types of dressing, that is)

Thanks to my friend Keith Fisher for this versatile, easy-to-prepare recipe that works equally well as a lunch salad or sandwich filling. Try it in a pita pocket for something extra special. White meat is preferable. Serves 2.

If using Romaine lettuce, wash, pat dry and tear to desired size. Place on serving plate(s) and chill until ready to use.

In a small bowl, combine ingredients for selected dressing and stir vigorously with a spoon until smooth.

Combine dressing with chicken salad mixture and serve atop Romaine lettuce or as a sandwich. Try a pita pocket!

Combine in a mixing bowl:

1¼ C. cooked chicken, preferably white meat

2 large uncooked carrots, roughly shredded

1 bunch seedless grapes (25–30 grapes total)

1 small apple, peeled, cored, and cubed (Gala or Braeburn)

½ C. walnuts, chopped

3–4 C. Romaine lettuce or bread/roll/pita for two sandwiches

Dressing:

¼ C. + 1 T. reduced fat mayonnaise

1 heaping T. white sugar

Sea salt and pepper, to taste

or:

3 T. rice vinegar

1 heaping T. white sugar

Sea salt and pepper, to taste

Sally Albright: I'd like the chef salad please with oil and vinegar on the side, and the apple pie a la mode.

Waitress: Chef and apple a la mode.

Sally Albright: But I'd like the pie heated, and I don't want the ice cream on top. I want it on the side, and I'd like strawberry instead of vanilla if you have it. If not, then no ice cream, just whipped cream, but only if it's real. If it's out of the can, then nothing.

Waitress: Not even the pie?
Sally Albright: No, just the pie, but then not heated.

When Harry Met Sally , MGM, 1989
Source: quotegeek.com

Keith's Hot Chicken Pasta Salad

Thanks again to Keith Fisher for another yummy, easy-to-make recipe. This one can be prepared with a variety of pastas and paired with a small green salad for a terrific brunch or light summer supper.

To Keith's tasty recipe, I enjoyed adding 2–3 T. of thinly sliced (reconstituted) sun-dried tomatoes. Try it if you're in the mood for a little extra zing. Serves 2–3.

---

4 C. cooked pasta (farfalle/bow-tie, fusilli, or small shells)

2 t. olive oil

2 medium yellow summer squash (or zucchini)

2 t. water

1 can (14 oz.) artichoke hearts, drained, rinsed and quartered

1½ C. cooked chicken, cut to 1" pieces

6 sprigs fresh parsley, chopped (or ½ t. dried parsley or cilantro)

Sea salt and pepper, to taste

½ C. fresh Parmesan, Romano or Asiago cheese, shredded

While pasta is cooking (al dente) according to package directions, heat olive oil over medium heat in large saucepan. Slice squash into ¼ inch rounds and add with water to saucepan. Cover and cook for 3–5 minutes (they should still be slightly crisp), stirring occasionally.

Add artichoke hearts and cubed chicken along with parsley, salt and pepper. Stir, cover and heat thoroughly, 2–3 additional minutes.

Serve immediately over well-drained, hot pasta with a liberal garnish of cheese.

Note: If adding sun-dried tomatoes, cut them into thin strips and add to saucepan with squash.

> Most vegetarians look so much like the food they eat that they can be classified as cannibals.
>
> — *Finley Peter Dunne (1867–1936)*
>
> Source: quotationspage.com

Chicken, Spinach and Feta Pinwheels

Light and fresh tasting, this recipe makes an excellent lunch or light dinner. Works well with any parts of the chicken, but white meat is preferable. Serves 4.

Combine all ingredients except tortillas in a large bowl and toss to mix well.

Lay out each tortilla and spread with one quarter of the chicken mixture. Distribute mixture evenly, leaving 1" margins at edge. Roll tortilla to create the pinwheel effect (similar to rolling a sleeping bag for storage) and seal by brushing water along the seam and pressing with fingers.

With a large sharp knife, trim away unfilled edges. Cut tortilla roll into 1" (or thicker) slices. Arrange on plates (perhaps on a bed of additional spinach leaves) and serve.

Variation: Layer thin-sliced ham over the tortillas prior to adding chicken mixture.

4 large (burrito size) flour tortillas (preferably a low-fat variety)

2 C. cooked chicken, shredded or diced

3 T. green onion, finely chopped

2 C. baby spinach (fresh, coarsely chopped)

½ C. fresh chunky salsa

1 T. extra virgin olive oil

½ C. crumbled feta cheese

½ C. mozzarella, finely shredded (or other white cheese)

Ground black pepper to taste

2 T. toasted pine nuts (optional)

> It is not the quantity of the meat, but the cheerfulness of the guests, which makes the feast.
>
> — *Edward Hyde*
>
> Source: quotegeek.com

Chicken Lentil Salad

This slightly spicy cold salad makes a nice brunch or light summer supper served on a bed of Romaine or your choice of salad greens. Try a double recipe for a colorful pot luck dish! Serves 6.

1 C. green lentils, rinsed and drained (Rinse with water in a small bowl. Discard anything that floats)

Water to cover lentils (add ½ t. salt to water)

½ t. rosemary, dried

2 t. tarragon, dried

¼ C. yellow bell pepper, seeded and diced

¼ C. red bell pepper, seeded and diced

3 T. green onions, minced

¼ C. extra virgin olive oil

2 T. balsamic vinegar

½ t. red pepper flakes

¼ t. sea salt

2 C. cooked chicken in small cubes or shredded

2 Roma tomatoes, seeded and diced

In a large skillet or wok over medium-high heat, combine lentils, rosemary, tarragon, green onion, bell peppers and enough lightly salted water to cover all. Bring to a boil then cover, reducing heat to low. Simmer 25 to 30 minutes, test for doneness, and drain. Set aside until ready to use.

In a medium bowl, use a fork to blend olive oil, balsamic vinegar, red pepper flakes and salt. Add cooked lentils and stir thoroughly, then gently fold in chicken and tomatoes. Cover and refrigerate at least 2 hours prior to serving.

▶ Serving Tip: Finished salad may be stored for up to 48 hours (but no more than four days from the date chicken was cooked).

> To make a good salad is to be a brilliant diplomatist—the problem is entirely the same in both cases. To know exactly how much oil one must put with one's vinegar.
>
> – Oscar Wilde
>
> The Nihilists, 1880

Couscous Chicken and Vegetable Pilaf

Inspired by a cooking class taught by noted Southern California chef Katherine Emmenegger, I adapted Katherine's low-fat recipe for use with cooked chicken. It's still low-fat and can be served warm, room temperature or cold, but remember to observe proper handling methods for chicken (see Reference section). Serves 6–8.

In a large stockpot or Dutch oven over medium-high heat, combine ½ C. of the chicken stock with red onion and garlic. Cook until onion is very tender, about 5 minutes. Add the zucchini and cook an additional 2–3 minutes.

Add remaining stock, asparagus, and tomato. Season with salt, pepper, and red pepper flakes.

Increase heat, bringing the mixture to a boil. Cover, reduce heat to medium and simmer until vegetables are crisp-tender, about 5 minutes. Add peas, chicken, and salsa. Mix thoroughly, and cook an additional 2–3 minutes. Add couscous, and remove from heat.

Replace cover and let stand 10 minutes. When ready to serve, fluff couscous with a fork, adjust seasoning and transfer to a large platter.

2½ C. chicken stock, divided

1½ C. red onion, diced

4 large cloves garlic, minced

1 medium zucchini, quartered and sliced

½ lb. asparagus (fresh or frozen) cut diagonally

1 large Roma tomato, seeded and diced

Sea salt and ground black pepper, to taste

¼ t. red pepper flakes, to taste

1 C. frozen petite peas

2 C. cooked chicken, cubed or shredded

1 C. fresh chunky salsa, drained (mild, with plenty of cilantro)

2 C. (uncooked) couscous

Spinach Salad with Orange-Spice Chicken

This light salad is a great change from the everyday, yet it's very fast to make. The chicken (white meat is preferable) can be made ahead and served hot or cold. Serves 2–3.

Dressing:
1½ t. sesame seeds, toasted in skillet or toaster oven

¼ C. orange juice

2 T. lemon or grapefruit juice

2 T. rice vinegar

1 clove garlic, minced

2 T. extra virgin olive oil

1 t. honey

1–2 t. cayenne red pepper sauce (optional)

Chicken and Glaze:
¼ C. + 1 T. orange juice

2 cloves garlic, minced

1 T. cayenne red pepper sauce

1 T. honey mustard (or 1 T. Dijon mustard + 1 t. honey)

1–1½ C. cooked chicken, white meat only

Salad:
5–6 C. spinach leaves, washed and dried

½ C. mandarin orange slices (drain if canned)

¼ C. + 1 T. crumbled feta cheese

Dressing: In a deep skillet (because you'll use it later for the chicken), place a few drops of olive oil and wipe with paper towel. Pre-heat skillet to medium and add sesame seeds. Keep seeds moving, about 2–3 minutes, to toast. Remove from heat and place seeds in a small bowl. Add juices, vinegar, garlic, oil, honey, and optional red pepper sauce, stirring to mix thoroughly. Set aside.

Chicken and Glaze: In the same skillet over medium heat, mix together juice, garlic, red pepper sauce and honey for glaze. Bring to a boil and simmer 3 minutes to reduce. Toss chicken in sauce to coat. Chicken should be well-coated but only warm in temperature.

Salad: Wash and spin dry or pat spinach leaves with paper towels. Dry leaves help salad hold dressing. Refrigerate until ready to use.

At serving time, place spinach leaves in a large serving bowl and toss with dressing.

To serve family style: Arrange glazed chicken on salad and surround with mandarin orange slices and crumbled feta. Serve promptly.

For individual portions: Toss mandarin orange slices and feta with spinach and dressing. Arrange salad on individual plates. Top each portion with chicken and serve promptly.

Summer Citrus Salad

I'm always impressed when my host makes salad dressing from scratch. You'll hear plenty of kudos for this one, and you don't have to admit how simple it was to make. The key to success is to make sure the lettuce is dry so that the dressing stays on the lettuce leaves. Serves 4–6.

Easy Citrus Vinaigrette Dressing

Citrus dressing adds a delightful tang to a salad that's both sweet and sour. This one came from Vincent Guerithault, chef/owner of Vincent's on Camelback in Phoenix. Vincent is known for his creative Southwestern cuisine served with good health in mind.

I prefer fresh juices, but high quality, not-from-concentrate packaged juice also tastes very good. Almost any citrus blend is wonderful, so feel free to experiment.

As close to serving time as possible, place greens, avocado, feta cheese and mushrooms in a large chilled mixing bowl. Toss with the citrus dressing, reserving 3 T. of dressing. Divide salad among 4–6 large plates and arrange chicken slices on top.

Drizzle remaining dressing over chicken and serve.

> The embarrassing thing is that the salad dressing is out-grossing my films.
>
> – Paul Newman
>
> Source: quotegeek.com

6–8 C. pre-packaged lettuce (Spring Mix or similar)

1 avocado, peeled and diced

1 C. brown mushrooms, cleaned and thinly sliced

½ C. feta cheese, crumbled (optional)

½ C. citrus vinaigrette (see below)

1½ C. cooked chicken, preferably white meat, cut to 1" cubes

In a 1 C. measuring cup, use a fork to blend together:

2–3 T. fresh lemon juice

2–3 T. grapefruit juice (Optional. Use additional orange juice or lime if omitting)

¼ C. fresh orange juice

1 t. honey

3 T. extra virgin olive oil

2 T. sherry wine vinegar (I often use balsamic vinegar)

1 T. chopped fresh cilantro (or 1 t. dried)

Sea salt and ground black pepper, to taste

Reduced Fat Florentine Chicken and Mushroom Quiche

This light, tasty quiche drastically lowers the fat content of its traditional cream-filled counterparts. Pair with a salad or fresh fruit plate to hold down the overall fat content of your meal. This recipe goes together in less than 20 minutes and bakes for 35. Serves 8.

Crust
9-in. pie shell, unbaked

Filling:
7 extra large eggs

¾ C. + 2 T. plain yogurt (whole milk or low-fat)

½ C. white onion, minced

½ C. Roma tomato, chopped

¾ C. fresh or frozen spinach, chopped

¼ C. fresh Parmesan cheese

1 C. cooked chicken (preferably white meat)

¼ t. sea salt

¼ t. ground black pepper

2 t. fresh or freeze-dried parsley

Crust: Pre-heat oven to 375°F. Let the refrigerated pie crust come up to room temperature for 15 minutes prior to using. When ready, fold out crust on a smooth, flat surface and match to size of pie plate or quiche pan. If necessary, roll the crust out slightly to enlarge it.

If using a pie pan, be sure to leave enough extra crust to flute the edge to discourage burning. Gently transfer crust to pan.

Filling: In a medium bowl, stir vigorously to blend eggs and yogurt. Use 6 eggs and ¾ C. yogurt for 9-in pie pan, or 7 eggs plus an extra 2 T. yogurt for a standard quiche pan.

Stir in remaining ingredients and pour into unbaked pie shell. Filling will expand slightly during baking. Bake 35 minutes or until filling is well set and lightly browned. It should be firm to the touch and a knife inserted in the center should come out clean. Serve hot.

California Classic Chicken Caesar Salad

Caesar salad originated in Tijuana, Mexico, but Chicken Caesar Salad is a "North-of-the-Border" creation. Homemade dressing is superior to anything you might buy, and it's actually very easy to make. The dressing recipe shown here is courtesy of LG's Prime Steakhouse. You can't get a Chicken Caesar Salad there, but you can enjoy a marvelous steak with a Caesar Salad prepared tableside whenever you visit the Palm Springs area. Serves 2–3.

Place anchovies and fresh garlic in a wooden salad bowl. Crush into a fine paste using the backs of two dinner forks (one in each hand). Add Dijon mustard and Worcestershire and stir. Add egg yolk and continue to stir.

While stirring continuously, SLOWLY add olive oil. Add lemon juice, red wine vinegar and half of the Parmesan cheese. Stir.

Place Romaine lettuce in dressing mixture and toss thoroughly, making sure to coat all sides of the lettuce leaves. Sprinkle with ground pepper, to taste.

Top with croutons, chicken and remaining Parmesan. Serve on chilled plates with chilled forks. Garnish plates or ring the outer edge of your salad with avocado slices, if desired.

Variation: Toss salad and chicken together and serve as a wrap inside whole wheat tortillas. Delicious!

10 oz. Romaine lettuce, chopped to 1"–2"

1 oz. anchovies (approximately 2)

4 cloves garlic, pressed (1 T.)

1 T. Dijon mustard

½ T. Worcestershire sauce

1 egg yolk

½ C. good quality extra virgin olive oil

1 t. lemon juice

2 T. red wine vinegar

¼ C. Parmesan cheese, freshly grated

1 C. seasoned croutons, preferably homemade

1½ C. chilled cooked chicken (white meat, cut into strips)

Freshly ground black pepper, to taste

Avocado slices to garnish (optional)

Marti's Oriental Chicken Salad

Who better to ask for a leftover cooked chicken recipe than Marti Naddaff, wife of George Naddaff, founder of Boston Chicken (known today as Boston Market)?

Marti writes, "I find that when I'm short of time, I often use a rotisserie chicken as the basis of a meal. They have made my life easier!" To make this recipe even simpler, she also suggests substituting commercially-prepared Chinese Chicken Salad dressing. Serves 6–8.

Also take a look at Stacy's Oriental Chicken Salad on page 62 for a variation on the same theme.

Dressing:

²⁄₃ C. soy sauce

½ C. rice vinegar

6 T. sesame oil

3 T. Chinese rice wine or sake

3 T. sugar

Salad:

Meat of 1 rotisserie chicken, shredded

1 head iceberg lettuce, torn into bite-sized pieces

1½ C. sliced green onions

1½ C. coarsely chopped, fresh cilantro leaves

2 C. fresh bean sprouts

4 carrots, coarsely shredded

1 C. sliced almonds

1 can (5 oz.) crispy chow mein noodles, optional

Dressing: In a medium bowl, combine dressing ingredients, stirring to dissolve sugar. Set aside. Makes about 2 cups.

Salad: In an extra-large bowl, combine all salad ingredients. Rice wine suitable for cooking is available in the Asian food section of many supermarkets.

Just before serving, add dressing and toss. Garnish with crispy chow mein noodles, if desired.

> While it's good to know how to cut up your own chicken, I often buy it cut up; because that way I can get all the dark meat I want. Looking at prices in the supermarket, you will see that chicken breasts are by far the most expensive per pound, and, according to me, they have the least flavor and the least satisfactory flesh quality. I choose chicken thighs for my sautés.
>
> — *Julia Child*
> *Julia and Jacques Cooking at Home*
> *Julia Child and Jacques Pépin, (2000)*
>
> Source: quotationspage.com

Chicken, Chicken and More Chicken Salad

This tasty chicken salad can be placed on a bed of romaine or leaf lettuce or spread on bread, toast or rolls for sandwiches. Use any combination of light and dark meat. Serves 3–4.

In a medium bowl, combine all ingredients, using a fork to mix well. Add a few drops of water if salad seems too dry.

Enjoy atop a fresh green salad or as a sandwich on a multi-grain roll or toasted bread.

2 C. chilled cooked chicken, shredded

3 T. white onion, finely chopped

2 T. celery, finely chopped

¼ C. low-fat mayonnaise

⅛ t. sea salt, to taste

¼ t. ground black pepper

1 T. lemon juice

2 T. slivered or shaved almonds

3 T. mandarin orange slices, chopped (canned)

> Noah Cross: I hope you don't mind, I believe they should be served with the head.
> J.J. Gittes: Fine, as long as you don't serve chicken that way.
>
> — *Noah Cross (John Huston), and J.J. Gittes (Jack Nicholson), Chinatown, as Gittes looks at the whole fish served to him for his meal (1974). Robert Towne, screenwriter.*
>
> Source: The Columbia World of Quotations. 1996.

Chicken and Feta Salad or Sandwich

Summer brunches never tasted so good! This salad blends the light taste of white meat chicken with the strong, smooth flavors of feta and cream cheese. Sliced tomatoes provide the perfect complement. Serves 2–3.

1½ C. cooked chicken breast

2 T. chives minced

1 C. feta cheese

½ C. cream cheese, softened (plain)

3 T. water

Sea salt, to taste

Freshly ground black pepper, to taste

1–2 large tomatoes (Beefsteak or similar), sliced

2–3 celery stalks, tops removed, sliced lengthwise (optional)

Combine chicken, chives, feta, cream cheese, and water in a mixing bowl and stir to combine. Add a few drops of additional water if mixture seems too dry. Add salt and pepper to taste.

For Salad: Place a generous portion of tomato slices on each salad plate (salt tomatoes if desired) and top with a mound of chicken salad. Garnish with celery stalks if desired.

For Sandwich: Dice tomatoes, filling pita bread with a combination of the chicken salad mixture and tomatoes.

> You don't have to cook fancy or complicated masterpieces — just good food from fresh ingredients.
>
> — *Julia Child*
>
> Source: quotationspage.com

Couscous Salad with Red Onion

Hot summer days were made for salads. This one is a great choice, because it provides the satisfying flavor of a home cooked meal without keeping you in the kitchen too long on a beautiful, sun-drenched day. This versatile salad can be a meal by itself, or pair it with a steaming bowl of Spinach and Tofu Soup (page 24) or a side of steamed broccoli. Serves 3–4.

Boil water for couscous. Meanwhile, pre-heat 2 T. of olive oil in a deep skillet over medium heat. Begin sautéing onions, bell pepper and tomatoes seasoned with salt and pepper until softened (4–6 minutes).

While vegetables sauté, add salt, couscous, and butter to boiling water. Stir to combine, remove from heat and cover tightly. Let rest for 5 minutes. Do not overcook. Uncover and stir after 5 minutes if not yet ready to use.

Add chicken and stock, followed by cooked couscous, to vegetable mixture. Stir to combine, and season with remaining ingredients, including additional salt and pepper, to taste. Cover and remove from heat until ready to serve.

Serve warm or at room temperature over a bed of field greens or romaine hearts, or simply serve family style in a colorful serving bowl.

1¼ C. water, boiling

1¼ C. whole wheat or regular couscous (uncooked)

2 T. butter

½ t. sea salt

2 T. olive oil, divided

1 large red onion, diced (about 1½ C.)

1 yellow bell pepper, diced (about 1 C.)

2 large Roma tomatoes, diced (about 1¼ C.)

Sea salt and freshly ground pepper, to taste

1½ C. cooked chicken, cut to bite size

1½ C. chicken stock (see page 14)

¼ t. ground red pepper flakes (optional)

3 T. fresh or freeze-dried basil, finely chopped

3 T. fresh lemon juice

3 T. rice vinegar

Microwave Philly Chicken Sandwiches

The secret to a great sandwich is great bread! I like these in French baguettes. A 6" length makes a perfect portion for one. For a flavorful and fast dinner, pair these sandwiches with the Tomato Leek soup shown on page 20.

French baguette or hoagie roll

Horseradish sauce

Cooked chicken breast, 3–4 oz. per sandwich (sliced as thinly as possible)

White cheese slices (white cheddar, Swiss, Monterey Jack)

Sliced red and yellow bell pepper

Sliced red onion

Slice the baguette into 6" lengths and again horizontally (but do not slice through). Spread horseradish sauce inside both bread halves. Add chicken slices, cheese, peppers and red onion.

Wrap each sandwich in a slightly damp paper towel and microwave 45 seconds to 1 minute on HIGH until cheese is slightly melted.

Enjoy sandwiches on their own or with soup, a fresh fruit plate, or salad.

> Fresh chicken skin can be white or yellow and is impacted by the chicken's diet. Yellow skin color is caused by a dietary ingredient found in marigold petals.
>
> In the U.S., chicken skin color varies by region in response to consumer preference and industry tradition. Chickens sold in the Northeast are more likely to be yellow-skinned, while skin of chicken sold in the South is more likely to be white.
>
> Source: USDA.gov

Toasted Chicken Sandwiches

These gourmet sandwiches make a terrific lunch. Pair with soup or a green salad for a fast and tasty dinner. Crusty gourmet bread makes this sandwich special. Monitor heat carefully and be patient so that sandwich can heat throughout without burning the bread.

While warming griddle or large flat skillet to medium heat, prepare sandwiches. Butter outside of bread lightly and spread honey mustard (or Dijon or both) inside both bread halves. Add chicken slices, cheese and optional ingredients.

Place sandwiches on griddle and cover loosely. Reduce heat if needed, monitoring carefully until brown.

Turn sandwiches and reduce heat to low. Cover more tightly and "slow roast" sandwiches until browned and heated through, approximately 4–5 minutes.

Enjoy with soup, fresh fruit plate or red potato salad. Be creative!

Variations: Try avocado slices, a few bean sprouts or spinach leaves (fresh, well-washed and patted dry).

Gourmet bread (such as spinach parmesan, sourdough)

Honey mustard or Dijon mustard

Butter

Cooked chicken, 3–4 oz. per sandwich (sliced as thinly as possible)

White cheese slices (provolone, white cheddar, Swiss)

Four places in the United States have the word "chicken" in their names: Chicken, Alaska; Chicken Bristle in both Illinois and Kentucky, and Chicken Town, Pennsylvania.

Chicken and Potato Hash
with Basted Eggs

Growing up in Western Pennsylvania, I would have called this diner food, but trendy breakfast restaurants serve similar fare as "skillet breakfasts." This is a great dish to make if you have leftover potatoes, but you can also start out with raw potatoes. You'll have to be patient, but they *will* brown. Both variations are shown below. Serves 2.

Hash: In a 10" or larger skillet over medium heat, preheat oil and add potatoes. Stir occasionally and reduce heat if necessary so that potatoes sauté gently (don't try to rush them). Brown potatoes 5–7 minutes or until golden, then add chicken stock, onion, bell peppers, mushrooms, and tomato.

Sauté until vegetables are soft, an additional 4–5 minutes.

If using bacon: While vegetables sauté, microwave bacon wrapped accordion-style in paper towels, approximately 3–4 minutes on high (bacon should be fairly crisp, but microwave cooking times vary).

Add chicken and crumbled cooked bacon. Sprinkle with Essence and salt or add similar seasonings. Stir to incorporate, and taste. Re-season if necessary and reduce heat to low.

Hash:

2 T. macadamia nut oil or extra virgin olive oil

2 C. cooked white, new or red potatoes, cubed (¾")

¼ C. chicken stock (see page 14)

½ C. white or yellow onion, chopped

¼ C. + 1 T. red bell pepper, diced

¼ C. green bell pepper, diced (optional)

½ C. brown mushrooms, thinly sliced

½ C. tomato, chopped (Roma, vine-ripe, etc.)

1 C. cooked chicken, diced

3 strips cooked bacon, crumbled (optional)

½ t. Emeril's Essence® (original flavor)*

Sea salt, to taste

Chicken and Potato Hash
with Basted Eggs

(continued)

Basted Eggs: In a 10" heavy non-stick skillet that can be tightly covered, heat oil or butter at medium (a skillet with a glass lid is best for monitoring eggs). Season the skillet using a paper towel to distribute and remove excess oil or butter. Ideally, drops of water added to skillet should sizzle gently.

Crack eggs on skillet edge and drop gently into skillet. Don't worry if edges run together. Quickly season eggs with salt and pepper. Add water at skillet edges (or any spots not covered by egg). Immediately cover to capture steam. Cook to desired doneness, about 2 minutes for runny yolks and 3-4 minutes to set yolks. Monitor carefully. If your pan lid isn't see-through, resist the urge to constantly lift, which lets the steam out. Add additional water, if necessary to maintain steam. When done, remove eggs from skillet immediately to avoid overcooking.

Final Preparation: While eggs cook, quickly arrange potatoes on warm plates or shallow serving dishes. Top with eggs and garnish, if desired, with sliced tomatoes or herbs.

Basted eggs:

1 t. additional macadamia nut oil or butter

4 extra large eggs

3 T. water

Sea salt, to taste

Freshly ground black pepper

*Emeril's Original Essence ingredients: salt, paprika, granulated garlic, black pepper, onion powder, whole thyme leaf, whole oregano leaf and cayenne pepper.

▶ *Cooking Tip: Uncooked potatoes are also great in this recipe. Be patient. It will simply take longer (about 15 minutes) for them to brown.*

Tri-Color Chicken Wraps

This simple-to-prepare recipe is full of strong flavors that will excite without overpowering. Use any type of tortilla or wrap you wish. Middle Eastern lavash bread (flat bread that resembles a large flexible soda cracker) is another option. Makes 4–5 wraps.

Dressing:
¾ C. low-fat plain yogurt

2 large garlic cloves, minced

2 T. fresh cilantro, minced (or 2 t. dried)

¾ t. ground cumin

1 T. lime juice

½ t. black pepper

Sea salt to taste

Wrap:
2 T. olive oil

3 bell peppers (green, yellow, red) seeded and cut into strips

1 large red onion, chopped

Sea salt and pepper, to taste

1½–2 C. chicken meat, cubed

½ t. cumin

Sprinkle of red pepper flakes

4–5 large tortillas or wraps (warm in microwave)

Dressing: Mince garlic and cilantro and place with yogurt in a small bowl. Blend in cumin, lime juice, and black pepper. Add sea salt, to taste. Cover and refrigerate until ready to use.

Wrap: In a large skillet over medium heat, pre-heat olive oil and sauté bell pepper and onion seasoned with salt and pepper. When vegetables are crisp-tender, about 4–6 minutes, add chicken and remaining seasonings. Blend thoroughly and continue to heat until chicken is hot.

Final Preparation: Prepare prior to serving or serve family style and let each person build his/her own: Place 2–3 T. of chicken mixture in each warm tortilla. Drizzle ¼ of dressing over each and fold tortilla up from the bottom and in from the sides to form a wrap. Serve immediately.

> Spike: There's something wrong with this yogurt.
>
> William: It's mayonnaise.
>
> Spike: Oh.
>
> — *Notting Hill*
>
> Source: quotegeek.com

The Basic Crepe

Crepes have evolved over centuries to serve as vessels for breakfast, lunch, dinner and dessert. Here, you'll find a crepe starter recipe with some suggested variations using cooked chicken. Pre-made crepes may be available refrigerated or frozen. Crepes may be made ahead and refrigerated for up to 3 days, or frozen for up to several weeks. Serves 4 (10–12 crepes).

Place ingredients in a large bowl or blender. Whisk or blend until very smooth, pausing to scrape down sides of bowl or blender. If using a bowl, start with the eggs and whisk, and then add other ingredients, incorporating liquid gradually to discourage lumps. Batter should be the consistency of thick heavy cream.

1 C. all-purpose flour

2 large eggs

½ C. milk (2%, whole milk or Soymilk)

½ C. water

½ t. sea salt

1 T. butter, melted

To Make Crepes: Use a crepe maker or a heavy 8" non-stick skillet. Heat skillet over medium heat and season by removing from heat and rubbing butter into the non-stick surface. You may need to repeat seasoning after every 3rd or 4th crepe.

Skillet is ready when water droplets skid on surface and evaporate slowly. Each crepe will require about 3 T. of batter. Use a ¼ C. measure to drop batter onto skillet and promptly swirl batter in skillet to distribute evenly. Brown crepe lightly then use a small spatula and your (clean) fingers to turn and brown the reverse side. Crepes made on a crepe maker generally do not require turning.

If using the same day or refrigerating, stack crepes on a plate. If freezing, use wax paper to separate layers. Repeat steps above, then set crepes aside or store until ready to use.

Two Great Crepes

The great thing about crepes is their versatility. They can be used in an incredible array of dishes. Notice that the filling starts out similarly both times but the variations are nearly endless. Here are two I particularly like. Each serves 4.

Chicken, Broccoli and Mushroom Crepe

¼ C. butter

½ C. white onion, diced

2 cloves garlic, minced

1 C. brown mushrooms

3 T. all-purpose flour

1½ C. milk (2%, whole milk, or soymilk)

1 C. chicken stock (see page 14)

1 C. small broccoli flowerets, (small bite size)

1½ C. cooked chicken

½ t. ground nutmeg

¾ C. Swiss or Monterey Jack cheese, shredded

Sea salt and black pepper to taste

Parmesan cheese to garnish

Preheat oven to 375°F

Filling: In a large saucepan over medium heat, melt butter and sauté the onion, garlic and mushrooms until soft. Sprinkle flour lightly over top and stir until smooth. Gradually add liquids and bring to a boil, stirring frequently until thickened, 4–5 minutes. Reduce heat to medium-low and stir in broccoli, chicken and nutmeg. Cover and cook 2 minutes more. Remove from heat and stir in cheese.

Final Preparation: Place at least ¼ C. of filling in each crepe. Roll and place seam side down in a greased 9" × 13" baking pan. Continue filling all crepes, reserving any extra sauce for serving. Bake uncovered 15 minutes or until heated.

When ready to serve, thin remaining sauce with milk if necessary (it should be the consistency of gravy to pour well). Serve 2–3 crepes per person topped with sauce and Parmesan.

Florentine Crepes

Filling: Preheat oven to 375°F. In a large saucepan over medium heat, melt butter and sauté the onion, garlic and mushrooms until soft. Add wine and simmer 2–3 minutes. Sprinkle flour lightly over top and stir until smooth. Gradually add liquids and bring to a boil, stirring frequently 3 minutes or until thickened. Stir in chicken and spinach. Cover and cook 2 minutes. Remove from heat and add cheese.

Final Preparation: Place at least ¼ C. of filling in each crepe. Roll and place seam side down in a greased 9" × 13" baking pan. Continue filling all crepes, reserving extra sauce for serving. Bake 15 minutes or until heated. Thin remaining sauce with milk if necessary (it should be the consistency of gravy to pour well). Serve 2–3 crepes per person topped with remaining sauce and a garnish of Parmesan.

Variations: Two More Ideas for Crepes:

• Stuff with chicken, crumbled hot sausage and scrambled eggs cooked with onion and bell pepper, similar to a breakfast burrito.

• Substitute tomatoes and asparagus pieces for broccoli and mushrooms in the first recipe.

3 T. butter

½ C. white onion, diced

2 cloves garlic, minced

¾ C. brown mushrooms

½ C. white wine

2 T. all-purpose flour

1½ C. milk (2%, whole milk or Soymilk)

½ C. chicken stock (see page 14)

2 C. cooked chicken (preferably white meat)

6–7 oz. frozen chopped spinach, defrosted and well-drained

1½ C. Swiss cheese, grated

Parmesan cheese or additional grated Swiss cheese to garnish

Which Came First???

According to *National Geographic*, scientists have settled the old dispute over which came first — the chicken or the egg. They say that reptiles were laying eggs thousands of years before chickens appeared, and the first chicken came from an egg laid by a bird that was not quite a chicken. That seems to answer the question. The egg came first.

Source: Knowledge in a Nutshell

Chicken and White Corn Mishmash

Janene Alford contributed this tasty Antiguan recipe which is great for brunch or a light supper. We worked together to enhance it with shredded cooked chicken and additional vegetables. Be creative and add whatever you have handy: zucchini, green bell pepper, maybe a few mushrooms, etc. Serves 4.

---

2 eggs, beaten (extra large or jumbo, otherwise use 3 eggs)

½ **C. bread crumbs (Italian style)**

1 can (4 oz.) mild green chilies

3 T. white onion, diced

3 T. red bell pepper, diced

1 can (11 oz.) white shoepeg corn (or similar white corn)

1 C. low-fat milk

1 t. dry mustard (or 1 T. Dijon)

1¼ **C. cooked chicken, shredded**

1 C. Monterey Jack or other cheese, shredded

Preheat oven to 350°F.

Spray a deep 2-quart casserole with cooking spray or coat with butter. In a large mixing bowl, combine beaten eggs and other ingredients, mixing thoroughly with a fork as ingredients are added.

Turn mixture into casserole and bake uncovered in a water bath for 60 minutes. It's done when the top springs back to the touch and is lightly browned. Casserole should pull away from the edges slightly and/or show slight cracks on top.

▶ *Cooking Tip: This recipe uses a water bath to prevent the casserole from drying out or browning at the bottom. To prepare, simply use a larger baking pan than your casserole (it must be at least 2" deep) and place approximately 1" of water in the pan. Set casserole in center of water bath and bake as directed.*

Note: If corn is frozen, defrost before using.

> Dark meat gets its color from myoglobin, a compound that holds oxygen in the muscles. Myoglobin is most concentrated in the legs and thighs since those muscles do the most work.
>
> Source: eatchicken.com

Thai-Inspired Chicken Wraps

These mildly spicy wraps are an easy treat. Makes 4 wraps.

In a large skillet over medium heat, pre-heat oil and sauté garlic, ginger and bell pepper. When vegetables are crisp-tender, about 4–6 minutes, add chicken and red pepper flakes.

In a small bowl, whisk together peanut butter, soy sauce, lime juice and sesame oil until smooth, and add to chicken mixture. Blend thoroughly and continue to heat until chicken is hot.

Final Preparation: Prepare prior to serving or serve family style and let each person build his/her own. Place ¼ of chicken mixture and lettuce in each warm tortilla. Fold tortilla up from the bottom and in from the sides to form a wrap. Serve immediately.

2 T. olive or peanut oil

2 cloves garlic

1 t. ginger root, minced

2 medium yellow bell peppers, sliced

1½ C. cooked chicken

½ t. red pepper flakes

3 T. peanut butter

2 T. soy sauce

2 T. lime juice

2 t. sesame oil

4 spinach wraps or plain tortillas, warmed in microwave

2 C. romaine or iceberg lettuce, washed, patted dry, and shredded

Some breeds of chickens can lay colored eggs. Yes, the Ameraucana and Araucana breeds of hen lay green or blue-hued eggs.

The chicken population of the world exceeds the human population.

Source: flashofbrilliance.info

Chicken-O-Mato

Inspired by the Crab-O-Mato appetizer I fell in love with as a teenager visiting a Fort Myers Beach seafood restaurant, this dish can be paired with a green salad as the entrée for a wonderful summer brunch. Serve cold, toasting only the English muffin, or finish in the broiler. Makes 6 halves.

Chicken Salad:

2½ C. cooked chicken, shredded

¼ C. green onions, minced

2 T. prepared horseradish sauce*

¼ C. reduced-fat mayonnaise

Dash of cayenne red pepper sauce

2 T. water

1 t. fresh lime (or lemon) juice

Sea salt and black pepper, to taste

At serving time:

6 Beefsteak® tomato slices

6 English muffin halves

Sprinkle of paprika to garnish

In a medium bowl, combine the chicken salad ingredients (white meat is preferable) and mix with a fork until thoroughly blended. Cover and chill until ready to use.

At serving time: Toast English muffin halves and place 1 tomato slice and one-sixth of the chicken salad on each half. Sprinkle tops lightly with paprika.

Serve cold or broil 3–5 minutes, monitoring carefully to warm salad without burning.

Variation: For larger parties, place small portions of chicken mixture on melba rounds. Omit the tomato, or top each appetizer with a grape tomato half. Serve cold or place under the broiler or in a toaster oven until heated. Makes about 36 small appetizers.

*To use prepared horseradish (which is stronger than horseradish sauce) reduce horseradish to 1 T. and increase water to 3 T.

Appetizers
and
Party Food

Hot Chicken Salad Party Dip

A higher fat version of this recipe appeared in *Favorite Recipes of Home Economics Teachers* (1964). This updated version reduces the fat by almost half without sacrificing taste. Try it at your next get together and watch it get devoured!

2 C. cooked chicken, diced

2 C. celery, diced

1 C. nuts (cashews, pecans, almonds or a mix), chopped

½ C. low-fat mayonnaise

½ C. chicken stock (see page 14)

¼ C. white onion, finely chopped

1½ T. Worcestershire sauce

2½ T. lemon juice

½ C. plain potato chips, crushed (use lower-fat baked chips)

½ C. barbecue potato chips, crushed

Hearty whole grain crackers or Melba rounds for dipping

In a large mixing bowl, combine all ingredients except potato chips. Transfer to a 2-qt baking dish. Sprinkle potato chips evenly over top. Bake for 20 minutes at 350°F. Serve hot and enjoy!

To reduce the fat content further: Substitute ½ C. whole milk yogurt and 1 t. honey for the mayonnaise.

► *Cooking Tip: Chicken salad will stay warm longer if served in the same dish used for baking.*

Cooked chicken leftovers will remain fresh for 3 or 4 days if refrigerated promptly and placed in a clean container with a tight lid. It's also safe to store rotisserie chickens in the containers they're purchased in, leaving meat on the carcass.

Source: usda.gov

Italian Chicken Crescent Roll-Ups

Get ready for the Pillsbury Bake-Off®! Is there a category for incredibly fast and easy? If so, this one wins every time. For appetizer portions, cut each dough triangle in half lengthwise and fill. For brunch or lunch, prepare full-size Roll-Ups. This tasty hot appetizer can be made several hours ahead and refrigerated prior to baking. Makes 16 appetizers.

Pre-heat oven to 375°F or as specified on package. In a medium bowl, combine all ingredients and mix thoroughly. Open crescents and separate dough triangles onto cookie sheet. Spoon chicken mixture onto dough in equal portions (approximately ¼ C. each for full size, 2 T. for appetizers.) Extra filling is great on whole grain crackers as an appetizer.

Roll dough triangles around chicken (large end to small) and space evenly on cookie sheet to promote even browning. Bake according to package directions or until golden.

1 package Pillsbury Crescents®

Chicken Filling:

1½ C. cooked chicken, shredded

¼ C. chicken stock (or substitute water; see page 14)

3 T. white onion, minced

½ C. ricotta cheese

1 t. cayenne red pepper sauce

1 T. fresh basil, chopped (or 1 t. dried)

¼ t. sea salt, to taste

¼ t. black pepper, to taste

> Part of the secret of success in life is to eat what you like and let the food fight it out inside.
>
> — *Mark Twain*
>
> Source: quotationspage.com

Greek Tortillas with Chicken and Feta

Flour tortilla shells baked and topped with Roma tomatoes, chicken, and feta provide superb color while giving this recipe a Greek feel. Slice like a pizza into 8 pieces for parties or quarter for quick family dinners. Makes 32 appetizers (4 tortillas).

1½ C. Roma tomatoes, chopped (about 4–5 tomatoes)

1 large red bell pepper, thinly sliced lengthwise

½ yellow bell pepper (optional), sliced lengthwise

½ C. black olives, pitted and sliced or finely chopped

¼ C. fresh chives, minced

2½ C. cooked chicken, diced

2 T. red wine vinegar

2 T. fresh basil (or 1 t. dry)

Sea salt, to taste

Black pepper, to taste

3 T. olive oil, plus additional oil for brushing tortillas

4 large flour tortillas (8")

1½ C. feta cheese, crumbled

Preheat oven to 425°F. In a large bowl, combine the tomatoes, peppers, olives, chives, chicken, vinegar, seasonings, and olive oil.

Lightly coat the tortillas on both sides with oil. A crumpled paper towel dipped lightly in oil works well if you don't have a brush. Place on a pizza stone or baking sheet on center oven rack, overlapping if necessary. Bake the tortillas until edges start to brown, 2–3 minutes. Turn the tortillas and bake 2–3 minutes longer to brown the reverse side.

Remove tortillas from the oven and top each with an equal amount of chicken mixture and feta cheese. Bake an additional 7–9 minutes. With a pizza cutter or sharp knife, cut each tortilla into four or eight slices. Serve immediately.

> In order to make an apple pie from scratch, you must first create the universe.
>
> — *Carl Sagan*
>
> Source: quotationspage.com

Fiesta Chicken-Bean Dip

A great party dip, this recipe comes together in no time. Try to make it within 2–3 hours of serving time for freshest taste and to avoid browning of the avocado.

In a bowl, mix chicken with 3 T. of lime juice. Let stand while making dip.

In another larger bowl (at least 2-quart), combine refried beans, ½ C. sour cream, half of taco seasoning and salsa. Spread bean mixture in bottom of a 2-quart casserole dish. Chop avocado and squeeze remaining lime over it to help prevent browning. Distribute evenly over bean mixture and top with chicken.

In the bowl you used for the chicken, combine remaining 1 C. sour cream with remaining taco seasoning. Stir until smooth and layer over chicken in casserole. Next, add one layer each of cheese, onion, and tomato. Sprinkle with sea salt and freshly ground black pepper. Top with black olives.

Chill until ready to serve. Serve with tortilla rounds or chips for dipping.

2 C. cooked chicken, diced or shredded

3 T. fresh lime juice, plus an additional squeeze

1 can (16 oz.) low-fat or fat-free refried beans

1½ C. low-fat sour cream, divided

1 package (1¼ oz.) dry taco seasoning mix, divided

3 T. fresh salsa

1 medium-large avocado, finely chopped

1 C. extra sharp cheddar cheese, shredded

½ C. white or green onion, finely chopped

2 Roma tomatoes, seeded and chopped

Sea salt, to taste

Ground black pepper, to taste

1 can (4.2 oz.) black olives, chopped or sliced

1 lb. bag tortilla rounds or chips

> Mr Green: Who would want to kill the cook?
> Miss Scarlett: Dinner wasn't that bad.
>
> — Clue
>
> Source: quotegeek.com

Stacy's Oriental Chicken Salad

Stacy Ottaviano, the youngest really good cook I know, contributed the recipe for this party-size salad that works deliciously with cooked rotisserie chicken.

Also take a look at Marti's Oriental Chicken Salad on page 42 for a very different exploration of the same theme.

---

4 C. cooked chicken

½ C. Teriyaki sauce (preferably Hawaiian style)

Salad:

6 C. fresh salad greens (50:50 iceberg and romaine is a nice mix

½ C. of celery, diced

4 green onions, including dark green tops

2 T. toasted sesame seeds

½ C. petite peas

¼ C. water chestnuts

½ C. mandarin orange slices

½ C. chow mein noodles to garnish (optional)

Dressing:

¼ C. + 2 T. sugar

½ t. ginger (or ¾ t. fresh ginger root, minced)

¼ C. + 1 T. sesame oil

¼ C. + 1 T. salad oil (canola or extra-virgin olive oil)

¼ C. rice vinegar

2 t. Dijon mustard

1 T. fresh lemon juice

Sea Salt and pepper to taste

In the refrigerator, marinate the cooked chicken in the sauce for at least a few minutes. This step may be done up to 48 hours in advance of making the rest of the salad.

▶ *Cooking Tip: An easy way to distribute the marinade evenly is to put it in a plastic bag with the chicken and shake.*

Combine salad ingredients except chow mein noodles in a large bowl and toss to mix. To toast the sesame seeds, try the dry skillet method outlined on page 12.

Combine dressing ingredients in a shaker cup and shake vigorously. Taste and adjust seasonings or sugar, if needed.

Close to serving time, add chicken, along with excess marinade (excess marinade is normally discarded, but since the chicken was already cooked, it's all right to use).

Pour dressing over salad, and toss to distribute. Top with chow mein noodles.

> I don't like food that's too carefully arranged; it makes me think that the chef is spending too much time arranging and not enough time cooking. If I wanted a picture I'd buy a painting.
>
> — *Andy Rooney*
>
> Source: quotegeek.com

Chicken Cheese Ball

A great alternative or addition to standard cheese and crackers, this cheese ball makes a festive dinner party hors d'oeuvre that can be made the day before and refrigerated until needed. Thanks to Lighthouse Foods (lighthousefoods.com) for contributing the original version. Serves 12–14. Make a half recipe for a smaller gathering.

Combine chicken, dressing, and cream cheese in a mixing bowl. Beat at low speed with an electric mixer until blended. Shape into two cheese balls or cheese logs.

Place nuts in a single layer on a large plate, and roll in pecans to coat. For elongated shapes, a few extra pecans may be needed. Toast pecans, if desired.

Cover and chill until needed. Serve with sturdy whole-grain crackers, bagel chips, or Melba rounds.

▶ *Cooking tip: Consistency and taste were best with "original" cream cheese (not low-fat, fat-free, or whipped versions.*

1½ C. cooked chicken, diced

¾ C. Litehouse® Ranch Dressing & Dip (any variety)

2 packages (8 oz.) cream cheese, softened

1 C. pecan pieces, chopped

"Poultry is for the cook what canvas is for the painter."

– Jean Anthelme Brillat-Savarin (1755-1826)

Source: Physiologie du Gout

Tuscan Chicken Cakes with Tomato-Basil Relish

The National Chicken Cooking Contest sponsored by the National Chicken Council and the U.S. Poultry & Egg Association seeks the best chicken recipe in the U.S.

Bob Gadsby of Great Falls, MT submitted the first winning recipe featuring pre-cooked chicken, winning the 44th annual contest.

Used with permission of the contest sponsors, here is the winning recipe (with a bit of additional explanation) followed by my version. Why not try them both?

---

3 C. cooked chicken, shredded and chopped

1 C. Italian seasoned bread crumbs, divided

¼ C. mayonnaise

1 egg, lightly beaten

¼ C. prepared basil pesto

2 t. honey mustard

⅓ C. finely chopped (prepared) roasted red peppers, drained

⅓ C. finely chopped red onion

2 T. olive oil

1 package (5 oz.) mixed salad greens

⅓ C. prepared balsamic vinegar and oil dressing

Golden Aioli:

½ C. mayonnaise

2 T. honey mustard

Whisk together in small bowl.

Tomato Basil Relish:

1 C. plum (Roma) tomatoes, seeded and chopped

⅓ C. red onion, chopped

3 T. sun dried tomatoes, chopped (soak 10 minutes and drain)

2 T. fresh basil leaves, slivered

2 T. prepared balsamic and oil salad dressing

1 t. prepared basil pesto

In a large bowl, mix together chicken, ½ C. of the bread crumbs, mayonnaise, egg, pesto, honey mustard, roasted peppers and red onion. Using a ⅓-cup measure, shape chicken mixture into 8 cakes; lightly coat each with remaining ½ cup bread crumbs. In a large nonstick frypan, pre-heat oil over medium-high heat. Add chicken cakes and cook until golden brown, about 3 minutes per side. Drain on paper towels. Toss salad greens with dressing and divide among 4 serving plates. Top each with 2 chicken cakes; drizzle with Golden Aioli. Top each cake with a dollop of Tomato-Basil Relish. Makes 4 servings.

My Favorite Chicken Cakes
Served Three Ways

I frequently serve Maryland style crab cakes and salad, so I began to wonder if I could make a similar dish using chicken, and found that the answer is "Yes." In fact, they're wonderful, but in testing the recipe, I found it best to enhance the chicken flavors rather than trying to imitate crab cakes. While still in the testing stage for this recipe, I stumbled across the Tuscan Chicken Cakes recipe shown earlier, and couldn't resist including both so that you can determine your favorite. This is yet another quick but very tasty meal you can make in less than 30 minutes. Makes 6 medium cakes.

Chicken Cakes:

2 T. extra virgin olive oil (or Macadamia nut oil)

1 egg, beaten

¼ C. chicken stock (see page 14)

2 T. milk (1%, 2% or whole) or half and half

¾ C. whole wheat saltines, crushed into crumbs

¼ C. + 1 T. green onion, minced

¼ C. celery, minced

1 t. sun dried tomato pesto

2½ C. cooked chicken

¼ C. prepared ranch salad dressing (reduced fat)

¼ C. fresh Parmesan cheese, shredded or grated

¼ t. ground cumin

Sea salt to taste

Serving Sauces:

Prepared marinara sauce

Heat 1 C. sauce and pour 2–3 T. over each cake)

Sour cream dipping sauce

In a small bowl, mix together:

½ C. prepared fresh salsa, drained (choose or make a salsa with plenty of fresh tomatoes and cilantro)

3 T. reduced fat sour cream

Chicken Cakes: Combine all ingredients except oil in a bowl, mixing well. Ingredients should hold together sufficiently to make patties. If not, add additional stock and/or 1 T. olive oil. With your hands or a tablespoon, form mixture into 6 firm balls and flatten balls into patties.

In a 10" skillet, pre-heat the olive oil and sauté patties 3–4 minutes per side until browned and thoroughly heated.

3 Variations:

- Serve alongside a field greens salad with fresh tomatoes and crumbled feta cheese.
- Top with a slice of provolone cheese or mozzarella during the last minute of cooking and serve topped with warm marinara sauce.
- Dip in a tangy sauce of salsa and sour cream

Chicken Quesadilla

Quesadillas can be served as either a quick appetizer or an entrée; be creative with your own variations. This basic recipe will get you started. Make it spicier (or milder) by varying the amount and type of salsa, or add a dash of red pepper flakes or cayenne red pepper sauce for extra spice. Delicious!

For each quesadilla:

2 large (7") flour tortillas (preferably a low-fat variety without lard)

¾ C. fresh chunky salsa (medium-hot)

¾ C. cooked chicken, shredded or thin-sliced

½ medium red bell pepper, chopped or thin-sliced

¾ C. Monterey Jack cheese or cheddar-jack blend, shredded

Garnish with ½ C. guacamole* and/or sour cream

Optional Ingredients:

• **Yellow or green bell peppers**

• **Spinach, chopped**

• **¼ t. red pepper flakes**

• **Black olives**

• **Fresh tomatoes, chopped**

• **Refried or black beans (reduce salsa)**

In a large flat skillet or griddle over medium-low heat, lay out the first tortilla and spread with salsa, as if making pizza. Top with remaining ingredients, distributing evenly. Lay the second tortilla on top and cover with a lid or foil to help hold in heat. Or use jumbo size tortillas, fill half, and fold over.

Heat 3–4 additional minutes on first side until tortilla begins to brown. Adjust heat if necessary. Once cheese melts (which helps hold the quesadilla together), turn it (see cooking tip) and brown the remaining side 4–5 minutes until thoroughly heated.

Remove from skillet and slice with a pizza cutter into 4, 6 or 8 pieces. Accompany with guacamole* and/or sour cream. Serve hot.

▶ *Cooking Tip: If you like the vegetables cooked a little more, start by sautéing them in 1–2 T. olive oil over medium heat. Set aside until needed. Proceed as above.*

*For a fast guacamole recipe, see page 10.

Main Dishes — Fast
(30 minutes or less)

Sweet and Sour Chicken

Need dinner on the table in less than 20 minutes? This recipe is for you! It's not only easy and fast, but tastes terrific. The strong flavors of this recipe perfectly complement thigh or leg meat, but breast meat works well too, especially when you lighten things up by using rice vinegar. Serves 4.

---

3 T. butter

2 cloves garlic, minced

1 t. oregano, dried

½ C. chicken stock (see page 14)

Juice of 1 lime (about 1½ T.)

¼ t. salt

½ t. black pepper

¼ C. apple cider vinegar or rice vinegar**

1 C. light brown sugar, firmly packed

3 C. cooked chicken, (dark meat preferred), cut to bite size

1 C. long grain rice

Begin by cooking rice according to package directions or in a rice cooker. You'll probably want to add rice to boiling water just before adding chicken below.

In a heavy saucepan over medium heat, melt butter and add garlic and oregano. Sauté 1 minute. Stir in remaining ingredients, except chicken. When sugar has melted, reduce heat to medium-low, stir in chicken meat, and cover skillet. Gently simmer for 8–10 minutes.

Stir chicken thoroughly, and cook uncovered for an additional 4–6 minutes, stirring occasionally, until chicken has absorbed sweet and sour flavors. Add additional chicken stock if mixture seems too dry. Serve over rice and enjoy!

**We tested both an organic apple cider vinegar (Trader Joe's®) and rice vinegar. Both versions were terrific, and tasters were split as to which was best. The cider vinegar produces a more robust, earthy flavor, while the rice vinegar version was lighter and more sweet. Why not try both?

Chicken and Broccoli Alfredo with Farfalle

Very good! Didn't add much salt because the chicken was seasoned

Because of the light texture of the Alfredo sauce, this is one of the few main courses in this book where white meat is preferable. The good news is that close measurement is NOT required for this recipe. Just adjust the milk up or down based on the amount of chicken, vegetables and pasta. Serves 3–4.

Boil water and cook pasta al dente according to package directions (add ½ t. sea salt to water, if desired).

While pasta is cooking, in a deep skillet over low-medium heat, melt butter and sauté garlic one minute. Whisk in flour to form a creamy paste (if you have non-stick cookware, be sure to use a non-metal whisk or use a non-metal slotted spoon).

Increase heat to medium, add milk ½ C. at a time, and continue to whisk to blend and thicken sauce (approximately 4–5 minutes). Switch to a spoon and stir in salt, pepper and Parmesan.

Add cooked chicken and reduce heat to low until chicken heats. Add steamed broccoli and cooked pasta. Continue to cook 1–2 minutes until all ingredients are hot. Stir in additional milk if mixture is too thick. Serve!

Variations: This recipe is also terrific with French cut green beans, petite peas, or a mix of petite peas and pearl onions (use fresh or frozen, not canned).

4–6 oz. cooked farfalle pasta (bow-ties)

2 T. salted butter

2 large cloves garlic, minced

2 T. all-purpose flour

2½ C. milk (2%, whole, or soymilk)

Sea salt, to taste

½ t. black pepper, to taste

½ C. shredded or grated fresh Parmesan

2 C. cooked chicken, bite size

2 C. broccoli (salted and steamed, but still very crisp)

peas are good!

Chicken and Asparagus Alfredo with Penne Pasta

A more elegant variation of the chicken and broccoli recipe, this mouth-watering recipe is very easy to prepare. It may be made with any parts of the chicken, but I prefer all or mostly white meat. Serves 3–4 (use 8 oz. pasta if 4).

6–8 oz. cooked penne (or similar "tube" pasta or rotini)

2½ T. salted butter

1 T. green onion, finely chopped

2 large cloves garlic, minced

2 T. all-purpose flour

2–2½ C. milk (whole, half-and-half or soymilk)

Sea salt, to taste

White pepper, to taste

2 C. cooked chicken (mostly white meat)

1½ C. asparagus cut to 2"–3" lengths (steamed, but still very crisp)*

½ C. grated fresh Parmesan or Italian blend cheese

Boil water and cook pasta al dente according to package directions (add ½ t. sea salt to water, if desired).

While pasta is cooking, in a deep skillet over low-medium heat, melt butter and sauté onion and garlic one minute. Whisk in flour to form a creamy paste (if you have non-stick cookware, be sure to use a non-metal whisk or use a non-metal slotted spoon).

Increase heat to medium and add milk gradually, continuing to whisk while blending and thickening sauce (approximately 4–5 minutes). Add salt and pepper. Cook 2 minutes. Add Parmesan and cooked chicken, reducing heat to low until chicken is heated.

Gently fold in par-cooked asparagus and cooked pasta. Cover and continue to stir occasionally until all ingredients are hot. Serve and enjoy!

*Purchase asparagus of uniform, medium thickness. Trim bottoms. Very thick stalks have a tendency to be tough or stringy. Too-thin stalks may overcook. Steam to 80% done (known as par-cooking).

Your Chicken Is Cooked

Southwestern Chicken Fettuccini

Creamy, spicy and to die for, this dish is fast and easy to prepare for one or a family. While effort was made to keep the fat to a minimum, this one really isn't on the dieters' recommended list, so if weight or cholesterol is an issue, turn the page. Serves 4.

While heating water for pasta, melt butter in a chef's pan or other pan (large enough to also hold sauce and cooked pasta). Add garlic and sauté 2 minutes.

Whisk in flour and then gradually add liquids (approximately ½ C. at a time), whisking frequently until smooth and thickened.

Stir in red pepper flakes, cilantro, green chilies and bell peppers. Bring to a boil, cover and simmer gently, 12–15 minutes until peppers are very soft. Add chicken and continue to heat, stirring frequently, 3–4 minutes or until pasta is ready.

Cook pasta in salted water to al dente according to package directions. Drain well. Add to sauce, toss and garnish with Parmesan. Serve hot and enjoy!

3 T. butter

2–3 cloves garlic, minced

3 T. all-purpose flour

1 C. half-and-half

2 C. chicken stock (see page 14)

½ t. red pepper flakes

1 t. cilantro leaves, dried (1 T. fresh)

1 can (4 oz.) green chilies (mild)

1 large yellow bell pepper (cut in strips)

1 medium red bell pepper (cut in strips)

2 C. cooked chicken

Sea salt and freshly ground black pepper, to taste

8 oz. fettuccini, preferably fresh

¼ C. Parmesan cheese to garnish

> Conversation is the enemy of good wine and food.
>
> — *Alfred Hitchcock (1899 – 1980)*
>
> Source: quotationspage.com

Artichoke Chicken with Fettuccini

When you're ready for a change from red sauces, this artichoke-laden sauce will be sure to please. If black olives aren't a favorite, simply reduce or omit them. Serves 4.

8–10 oz. fettuccini

3 T. extra virgin olive oil

3–4 cloves garlic, minced

1 C. brown mushrooms, thinly sliced

½ C. dry white wine or vermouth

¼ C. low-fat evaporated milk

1 C. chicken stock (see page 14)

2 T. cornstarch mixed with ¼ C. water

¾ bag (9 oz.) frozen artichoke hearts*

2 C. cooked chicken, sliced or cubed into 1"–2" pieces

Small can (4 oz.) black olives, pitted and sliced

Sea salt and ground black pepper, to taste

½ C. shredded fresh Parmesan or Asiago cheese to garnish

Cook pasta in salted water to al dente, according to package directions. Delay this step if pasta is fresh.

While heating water for pasta, heat oil over medium heat in a pan large enough to hold sauce and cooked pasta. Sauté garlic 1 minute. Add brown mushrooms and sauté an additional 3–5 minutes until tender.

Stir in chicken stock, wine and evaporated milk. Use a whisk to incorporate cornstarch mixture, increasing heat to simmer. Add artichokes and continue to cook an additional 7–8 minutes, stirring occasionally until artichokes are soft. Taste and season with salt and pepper.

Optional: Using a hand blender, purée sauce to desired consistency. Be careful to keep blades submerged to avoid splashing hot liquid!

Add chicken meat and black olives. Simmer 3–4 minutes until thoroughly heated.

Gently add drained pasta to sauce, making sure pasta is well-coated.

Remove pasta to a serving bowl or individual bowls. Garnish generously with shredded cheese and enjoy immediately.

*Or substitute one 14 oz. can of artichokes, drained

Spicy Chicken and Salsa Pasta

Spicy and satisfying, this is a great meal to toss together when you're in a hurry: It will be on the table in less than 20 minutes. Any tubular pasta or even small shells work well in this recipe. Serves 4.

Cook pasta in salted water to al dente according to package directions.

While heating water for pasta, heat oil over medium heat in a pan large enough to also hold sauce and cooked pasta. Sauté garlic 1 minute.

Stir in tomato, red pepper and thyme, and sauté an additional 3–4 minutes. Add salsa, chicken stock and beans, bringing the mixture just to a boil while stirring constantly. Taste, and add a pinch of salt, if desired.

Add chicken and continue to stir frequently, 3–4 minutes or until pasta is ready. Gently toss drained pasta with sauce making sure pasta is well-coated.

Remove pasta to a serving bowl or individual bowls. Garnish with cheese and serve immediately.

12 oz. rigatoni (cooked in salted water)

1 T. extra virgin olive oil

5 large cloves garlic, minced

1 Roma tomato, chopped

½ C. red pepper, chopped

1 T. fresh or 1 t. dried thyme

12 oz. fresh chunky salsa with cilantro (mild-medium)

½ C. chicken stock (see page 14)

½ C. white kidney beans (rinsed and drained)

Sea salt, to taste

1 C. cooked chicken meat, bite size

½ C. shredded Mexican cheese

> When you don't have any money, the problem is food. When you have money, it's sex. When you have both, it's health. If everything is simply jake, then you're frightened of death.
>
> — *J.P. Donleavy*
>
> Source: quotationspage.com

Chicken Bruschetta

What could be better than pasta with tomatoes and garlic? Add evaporated milk and you'll find out. This is an ultra-quick, ultra-tasty meal you can make in 10–15 minutes. Tubular pastas also work well here, including rigatoni or penne. Serves 2.

4–5 oz. angel hair pasta (cooked in salted water)

1 T. extra virgin olive oil

2 cloves garlic, minced

1 can (14 oz.) Italian style peeled, diced tomatoes*

¼ C. evaporated milk (whole or low-fat)

1 t. sun dried tomato pesto or 2 T. reconstituted sun dried tomatoes, chopped

1¼ C. cooked chicken, bite size

Shredded or grated fresh Parmesan to garnish

Cook pasta in salted water to al dente according to package directions.

While heating water for pasta, heat oil over medium heat in a chef's pan (or other pan large enough to also hold sauce and cooked pasta) and sauté garlic 1 minute.

Stir in tomatoes, evaporated milk, and pesto, and heat to simmering.

Add chicken and continue to heat, stirring frequently, 3–4 minutes or until pasta is ready.

Drain pasta and toss with sauce. Garnish with fresh Parmesan and serve immediately.

*We tested with S&W Ready-Cut® & Hunt's® brands

> Our minds are like our stomachs; they are whetted by the change of their food, and variety supplies both with fresh appetites.
>
> — *Quintilian (Rome, approximately 80 A.D.)*
>
> Source: quotationspage.com

Chicken and Red Pepper Fettuccini

Not the same old marinara sauce, this dish gets a kick from fresh red peppers plus plenty of chunky tomatoes and other healthy veggies. Using pre-made pasta sauce, this is a 30-minute meal that tastes as if it took all day. Serves 3–4.

In a large stockpot, bring 3 quarts of salted (¾ t.) water to a boil for pasta. While water is heating, prepare sauce.

Using a 3-quart chef's pan, saucepan, or wok, bring pasta sauce to a simmer over medium-high heat. Reduce heat and add remaining ingredients (except Parmesan cheese) in the order presented here. Simmer, stirring occasionally, and proceed to cook fettuccini or other pasta.

When salted water reaches a rolling boil, add pasta and cook according to package directions to al dente. Drain and add to sauce, tossing to coat. Let simmer 1 minute then serve in pasta bowls with a garnish of Parmesan cheese.

*Tomato Basil flavor sauce is not recommended

8 oz. fettuccini

1 jar (26 oz.) of your favorite prepared marinara sauce*

1 large red bell pepper, seeded and chopped

2 Roma tomatoes, diced (1 C.)

½ C. fresh spinach, chopped

½ T. cilantro, dried

¼ C. Ricotta cheese (part skim)

2 C. cooked chicken

Fresh Parmesan cheese to garnish (optional)

> If more of us valued food and cheer and song above hoarded gold, it would be a merrier world.
>
> — *J.R.R. Tolkien*
>
> Source: brainyquotes.com

Chicken and Asparagus Stir Fry

Chicken complements so many vegetables. Fresh asparagus is a great choice, as well as zucchini, broccoli, or frozen petite peas. Serves 3–4.

---

2 C. long grained rice (uncooked)

2½ T. extra virgin olive oil

½ C. green onion, finely chopped

2–3 large cloves garlic, pressed and minced

1 T. cornstarch mixed with ½ C. chicken stock (see page 14)

1½ C. thin asparagus cut to 1"–2" lengths

½ C. red bell pepper, seeded and cut to thin slices

Sea salt, to taste

Freshly ground black pepper, to taste

2 C. chicken meat, bite size

½ C. grated fresh Parmesan or Italian blend cheese

Steam rice according to package directions (add ¾ t. sea salt to water, if desired.

Meanwhile, pre-heat oil over medium heat in a wok or deep skillet. Sauté onion and garlic one minute. In a separate container, use a fork to whisk together cornstarch and stock. When smooth, stir into wok mixture.

Increase heat to medium-high and add asparagus, red bell pepper, and seasonings. Cook 2–3 minutes. Add cooked chicken, cover and reduce heat to low until chicken is heated and vegetables are cooked to your preference. Serve hot over rice.

*Purchase asparagus of uniform, thin to medium thickness. Trim and remove bottoms. Very thick stalks have a tendency to be tough or stringy.

> There is no love sincerer than the love of food.
>
> — *George Bernard Shaw*
>
> Source: quotationspage.com

Quick and Easy Chicken & Dumplings

This light version of a traditional favorite uses a lot less fat than your grand-mother probably used. Any combination of white and dark meat works well. Serves 4.

In a chef's pan, or deep skillet, heat chicken stock over medium-high heat until simmering. While stock heats, whisk together milk and flour in a small bowl until smooth. Reduce heat to medium and add flour mixture to stock, stirring frequently, approximately 8–10 minutes, until gravy begins to thicken. Add salt and pepper to taste. Stir in vegetables and chicken.

In a small bowl (feel free to use the same bowl as the flour mixture) gently blend together Bisquick and milk, just until a soft dough forms. Do not over-mix, or dumplings will be chewy!

Drop dough by rounded spoonfuls (4–6) into chicken mixture. Dough will double in size as it cooks, so space accordingly. Sprinkle lightly with paprika, if desired.

Reduce heat to low and cook uncovered 10 minutes, then cover and cook an additional 10 minutes. Serve steaming hot!

2½ C. chicken stock (see page 14)

¾ C. evaporated milk (or whole milk), cold

¼ C. whole wheat or all-purpose flour

1 C. frozen petite peas and pearl onions

½ C. fresh baby carrots, quartered lengthwise

2 C. cooked chicken, bite-size

Sea salt, to taste

White pepper, to taste

Dumplings:

1 C. low-fat baking mix such as Bisquick®

¼ C. + 2 T. milk

Sprinkle of paprika (optional)

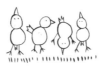

Chicken Pasta Primavera in Cilantro Garlic Butter Sauce

If you want to kiss anyone after eating this dish, make sure they have dinner with you. This dish is very tasty, but although it may be lower in fat than comparable recipes, it isn't low-fat. For a lower fat alternative, see the next page. Serves 2.

4 oz. penne or other favorite pasta

6 T. butter

4 large cloves garlic, crushed and minced

3 T. flour

2 C. chicken stock (see page 14)

1½ T. fresh or 2 t. dried cilantro leaves

1½ T. fresh lemon juice

Sea salt to season vegetables

1 C. broccoli, cut to bite size pieces

¾ C. baby carrots, quarter or halve lengthwise

¾ C. zucchini, cut 1" slices and quarter or halve lengthwise

¾ C. yellow squash, cut 1" slices and quarter or halve

1 C. Roma tomato, seeded and cubed (add to steamer last)

2 C. cooked chicken, bite size

Heat salted water for pasta and cook al dente according to package directions.

Melt butter in a deep skillet or chef's pan (large enough to hold pasta) over medium heat, and sauté garlic 1 minute. Whisk in flour to make a paste and then gradually whisk in chicken stock, stirring often as it thickens and comes to a boil. Add cilantro and lemon juice, and reduce heat. Simmer gently until vegetables are ready.

Steam seasoned vegetables while stock thickens. The idea is to cut pieces that will require the same cooking time. Steam the vegetables to 80% done – they will continue to cook when added to the pasta.

Stir in cooked chicken and vegetables followed by pasta, tossing to coat evenly. Serve hot and enjoy!

> If people let government decide what foods they eat and what medicines they take, their bodies will soon be in as sorry a state as are the souls of those who live under tyranny.
>
> — *Thomas Jefferson*
>
> Source: quotationspage.com

Low-Fat Chicken Pasta Primavera

This lower-fat pasta primavera will knock your socks off with flavor. Feel free to add additional vegetables or substitute your favorites. Serves 4.

In a deep skillet or chef's pan (large enough to hold pasta and vegetables) heat olive oil and butter over medium heat, and sauté garlic and onion 2–3 minutes.

Add wine or chicken stock (or pan drippings from the chicken container) and the brown mushrooms and bell pepper. Sprinkle with sea salt and sauté over medium heat approximately 5–7 minutes until soft.

While vegetables sauté, boil salted water for pasta. Cook pasta until al dente. Try to time pasta so that it can go right into the sauce.

Start broccoli (steam it or microwave with 2 T. water). Add as directed below.

Reduce heat to low, and stir in evaporated milk. Also add tomatoes and cooked chicken. Simmer the sauce over low heat while the pasta and broccoli finish. Sprinkle with additional salt and black pepper, to taste.

Drain the pasta, and add it to the sauce along with broccoli. Mix well. Transfer to serving bowl. Sprinkle with Parmesan, and serve.

Variations: Try sun dried tomatoes, zucchini, red bell peppers, or baby carrots.

8 to 10 oz. fusilli (corkscrews), penne or other favorite pasta

2 T. extra virgin olive oil

1 t. butter

4 large cloves garlic, crushed and minced

1 C. onion, coarsely chopped

¼ C. dry white wine, pan drippings, or chicken stock (see page 14)

2 C. brown mushrooms, sliced or quartered

1 yellow bell pepper, chopped

1 C. broccoli flowerets, steamed

1 can non-fat or low-fat evaporated milk, 8 oz.

1 large Roma tomato, seeded and chopped

1½–2 C. cooked chicken

Sea salt and ground black pepper, to taste

½ C. Parmesan cheese to garnish

Sesame Chicken Stir-fry

Stir frying is a fast and healthy way to cook. This dish combines a variety of flavors and textures to produce a flavorful meal with universal appeal. Sesame oil is the secret ingredient that ties everything together. A little goes a long way! Serves 4.

3 T. rice vinegar

2½ T. soy sauce

1½ T honey

1½ t. fresh ginger, grated

1 T. sesame oil

2 T. peanut oil

2 garlic cloves, minced (or 2 t. freeze-dried garlic)

2½ C. broccoli flowerets

¾ C. brown mushrooms, sliced

1 can (6 oz.) sliced water chestnuts, drained

2½ C. cooked chicken, bite size

2 T. toasted sesame seeds

In a small bowl, combine rice vinegar, soy sauce, honey, ginger, and sesame oil. Set aside until ready to use. Also be sure chicken is ready to use and toast sesame seeds prior to starting the stir-fry.

Heat peanut oil in a wok or large skillet over medium-high heat. Stir-fry garlic for several seconds. Add broccoli and mushrooms, and stir-fry until broccoli is crisp-tender, about 2–3 minutes. Stir in water chestnuts.

Add soy mixture to wok and also stir in chicken.

Continue to stir-fry, 2–3 minutes until chicken is thoroughly heated and broccoli is desired doneness. Sprinkle with toasted sesame seeds.

Serve over hot rice.

Wine pairing: Pinot Grigio or Pinot Noir

Chicken leads all meats in consumption, with 35% of the total consumption of beef, pork, poultry and fish/seafood.

courtesy of eatchicken.com

Chicken and Penne with Vodka Sauce

You can't get drunk from it, but you can savor the wonderful aroma and taste that the vodka provides. Serves 4.

In a 4-quart or larger saucepan bring salted water to a boil and cook pasta, al dente. If ready early, rinse to cool, drain well, and set aside until ready to use.

While water is heating for pasta: In a large skillet or chef's pan, heat the oil over medium heat and sauté the garlic with the red pepper flakes 1–2 minutes. Add tomatoes and carrots, continuing to simmer (uncovered) 15 minutes until sauce begins to thicken, stirring often. Remove carrots and discard them.

Add chicken meat and cilantro plus salt, to taste. Stir in milk and reduce heat. Add pasta and continue to cook 2–3 minutes over low heat, stirring frequently. Add vodka. Toss. Serve.

8–10 oz. penne (or substitute any similar pasta)

1 T. extra virgin olive oil

4 garlic cloves, minced (or pressed directly into pan)

½ t. crushed red pepper flakes

1 can, (28 oz.) crushed stewed tomatoes (Italian style)

12 baby carrots, halved lengthwise

2 C. cooked chicken

1 t. cilantro

Sea salt, to taste

¼ C. evaporated milk, whole or low-fat

¼ C. vodka (or try pepper vodka)

> I cook with wine. Sometimes I even add it to the food.
>
> — *W.C. Fields*
>
> Source: brainyquotes.com

Chicken and Rigatoni in Simple Sauce

It doesn't get much easier than this. Chicken is heated in olive oil, then tossed into freshly cooked pasta. Add cheese and you have a satisfying yet ultra-fast meal for one or a crowd. Serves 4.

---

10 oz. rigatoni (or other tube pasta cooked in salted water)

2 T. extra virgin olive oil or butter

3 large garlic cloves, pressed and minced

2 C. cooked chicken, bite size

1 T. chopped fresh basil or cilantro (or 1 t. dried)

Freshly ground black pepper to taste

3 T. additional extra virgin olive oil

½ C. Parmesan cheese, shredded or grated (fresh)

Boil pasta in salt water according to package directions. Cook just to al dente.

While pasta cooks, in a large saucepan, melt butter and sauté garlic 1–2 minutes. Add cooked chicken and seasonings, stirring until chicken is heated.

Drain freshly cooked pasta in colander and transfer to saucepan. Add olive oil and cheese, tossing to coat pasta evenly. Transfer to heated bowl (see cooking tip) and serve immediately. Delicious!

▶ *Cooking Tip: Pasta will stay hot at the table longer if served in a pre-heated serving bowl. Place the serving bowl you intend to use in the sink under your colander. The hot pasta water will quickly warm the serving bowl as the pasta drains.*

Herbs and spices that go well with chicken include ginger, marjoram, sage, thyme, rosemary and tarragon.

Courtesy of eatchicken.com

Spicy Chicken and Bell Peppers over Couscous

This spicy dish is especially terrific in colder weather and will perk up any gathering. Great as a fast dinner or prepare a day ahead and refrigerate to bring out even more complex flavors. Serves 4.

In a 3-quart (or larger) saucepan, heat oil and sauté bell pepper and onion seasoned with salt and pepper until soft (3–4 minutes). Increase heat to medium-high and add stewed tomatoes, cayenne red pepper sauce, and Worcestershire. **Caution: this dish gets spicier as it cooks!**

Add chicken. Taste and add more red pepper sauce if desired. Bring to a boil and reduce heat to continue simmering. Simmer at least 15 minutes and serve or continue to simmer up to an hour. Prepare couscous according to package directions 5 minutes prior to serving.

To serve: Place approx. ½ C. cooked couscous in a shallow pasta dish or on a plate. Spoon chicken and pepper mixture over couscous. Serve piping hot!

Variations: Try adding 1 medium yellow bell pepper, chopped, or 1 small can (3.5 oz.) diced green chilies (mild). Add along with vegetables.

Wine pairing: Try a spicy Alexander Valley Red Zinfandel.

1 T. olive oil

1½ C. red bell pepper, chopped

1 C. green bell pepper, chopped

½ C. white onion, diced

Sea salt, to taste

½ t. black pepper

1 can (28 oz.) crushed stewed tomatoes (plain or Mexican style)

2–4 T. cayenne red pepper sauce, to taste

1 T. Worcestershire sauce

2½ C. cooked chicken, bite size

1 C. (uncooked) couscous

Chicken Fried Rice

Very easy to make, fast, flavorful and nutritious. What more could you ask? This is a "starter" recipe, and your own creativity will aid you in trying variations. Try whatever you have in the refrigerator or freezer that sounds good! See the Cooking Tip for some tasty variations. Serves 3–4.

---

2 T. macadamia nut or peanut oil

1–2 cloves garlic, minced

¼ C. green onion, diced (including dark green tops)

½ t. gingerroot, peeled and minced

½ C. petite peas

¼ C. broccoli, diced

½ t. sugar

2 T. soy sauce, to taste

¼ C. water or chicken stock (see page 14)

2 C. (cooked) long grain white rice

1 C. cooked chicken, chopped

2 eggs, beaten

Pinch of salt (add to eggs prior to cooking)

½ t. sesame oil

If using a wok (preferred method): Heat oil to medium heat and sauté the garlic, onion and gingerroot, stirring constantly, 1 minute.

Increase heat to medium-high and add peas, broccoli, sugar, soy sauce and water or stock. Stir-fry 2 minutes, again stirring constantly.

Add cooked rice and chicken; stir-fry an additional 30 seconds. Make a well in center of wok (pushing ingredients to cool sides) and add eggs. Allow to set, then break up with spatula and stir into rice mixture. Add sesame oil. Serve immediately.

If using a skillet: Heat oil to medium heat and sauté the garlic, onion and gingerroot, stirring constantly. Add eggs (with a pinch of salt) and scramble, using a spatula to break up mixture as it begins to set.

Increase heat to medium-high and immediately add peas, broccoli, sugar and soy sauce. Stir-fry 2 minutes. Add rice and chicken, stir-fry an additional 1 minute. Add sesame oil. Serve immediately.

▶ *Cooking Tip: This is an "everything but the kitchen sink" recipe. Asparagus, any color of bell pepper, zucchini or other vegetables, either fresh or leftover, will add flavor and texture. Speaking of leftovers, that 2-day old rice leftover from Chinese take-out will be fine here. Add 2 T. of water, stir and use leftover rice as directed.*

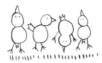

Chicken and Pasta Alfredo with Artichokes and Tomatoes

Adapted from a vegetarian recipe, this creamy combination is quick to make, but tastes as if you spent the afternoon in the kitchen. If you don't have farfalle, substitute almost any small tubular pasta. Serves 4.

In a large chef's pan or saucepan, melt butter and sauté garlic and onion over medium heat for 2–3 minutes. Sprinkle with flour, stirring with a whisk to incorporate. Add wine and simmer 2–3 minutes until wine is noticeably reduced.

Meanwhile, bring water to a boil, and cook pasta according to package direction. Time pasta to finish cooking just after sauce is ready.

Gradually stir in milk (½ C. at a time), continuing to whisk as sauce thickens (approximately 5 minutes). Add chopped artichokes and artichoke liquid to pan as well as tomatoes (to substitute frozen artichoke hearts, defrost prior to using and also add ½ C. chicken stock). Gently simmer 4–6 minutes.

Add chicken and cook an additional 3–4 minutes until chicken is thoroughly heated and vegetables are desired doneness. Stir in chopped basil and season to taste with salt and pepper. Add additional milk if sauce is thicker than desired.

Add cooked pasta to sauce and toss to coat pasta evenly. Serve hot with a garnish of cheese and enjoy!

Ingredients:

- 2 T. butter
- 2 cloves garlic, pressed and minced
- ¾ C. white onion, diced
- 2 T. flour
- ½ C. medium dry white wine (or increase chicken stock; see page 14)
- 8 oz. farfalle or bow-ties
- 2 C. milk (2%, whole or soymilk)
- 1 can (8 oz.) artichoke hearts, with liquid, cut to small pieces
- 1½ C. Roma tomatoes, diced (about 3 large tomatoes)
- 1½ C. cooked chicken
- Sea salt, to taste
- Freshly ground black pepper, to taste
- 2–3 T. fresh chopped basil (2–3 t. dried)
- ½ C. fresh Parmesan cheese to garnish

Quick and Easy Chicken Enchiladas

An "off the shelf" fast dinner, simply open a few containers, assemble the enchiladas and bake. Dinner is served! Serves 5–6 (two tortillas per person).

---

4 C. cooked chicken, shredded

16 oz. fresh chunky salsa (medium-medium hot)

½ C. small curd cottage cheese

1 can (4 oz.) diced green chilies

3 C. (¾ lb.) Monterey Jack or Mexican cheese blend, shredded

1 can (14 oz.) red enchilada sauce

10–12 medium corn tortillas (two per person)

½ C. sliced black olives (optional)

3 green onions, minced, including dark green tops

Low-fat sour cream, additional salsa and avocado slices or guacamole* to garnish

Pre-heat oven to 375°F.

In a large bowl, combine the chicken, salsa, cottage cheese, chilies, and half the cheese.

Pour half of enchilada sauce in the bottom of casserole and begin with one tortilla at a time. Fill each tortilla with ¼ cup chicken mixture. Roll to close and place tortillas seam side down in casserole.

Top with remaining enchilada sauce, olives (if desired), green onions, and cheese. Bake for 20–25 minutes at 375°F or until heated and bubbly.

Serve with a garnish of fresh avocado slices or guacamole, sour cream, and salsa.

*See page 10 for a fast guacamole recipe

Approximately 8 billion meat chickens will be raised in the United States this year — that's about one-third of the world's total.

Source: eatchicken.com

Fast Chicken and Noodles Skillet Meal

This dish provides comfort food for a fast family dinner that tastes just like grandma might have made. Serves 4.

In a large, deep skillet, slowly sauté the onion and mushrooms in olive oil until softened, 8–10 minutes.

Increase heat and add chicken stock, bringing mixture to a boil. Season with salt and pepper and add noodles, continuing to simmer 11–12 minutes or until noodles are tender.

Add chicken meat to skillet along with broccoli. Reduce heat to low and cover, stirring occasionally until ready to serve.

1½ T. olive oil

1 medium sweet onion, chopped (1 C.)

¾ C. brown mushrooms, sliced

3 C. chicken stock (see page 14)

Sea salt, to taste

½ t. freshly ground black pepper, to taste

8 oz. thin egg noodles (uncooked)

2 C. cooked chicken

Optional Ingredient:

1 C. broccoli flowerets (lightly season with salt and microwave with 2 T. water or steam to 75% done prior to adding to skillet)

Heywood Floyd: What's that, chicken?

Michaels: Something like that. Tastes the same, anyway.

— *Heywood Floyd (William Sylvester) and Michaels (Sean Sullivan), 2001: A Space Odyssey, discussing synthetic food served on spaceships (1968). Screenwriter: Stanley Kubrick*

Source: The Columbia World of Quotations. 1996

Chicken and Mushroom Risotto

This beautiful and tasty risotto is easy to make and can be on the table in less than 30 minutes if you make the chicken stock ahead. Serve with a steamed green vegetable for wonderful color and to create a well-balanced meal. Serves 4.

4 C. heated chicken stock (see page 14)

1½ T. butter

1 medium onion, chopped

2 cloves garlic, pressed and minced

1½ C. (4–5 oz.) brown mushrooms, sliced

1½ C. Arborio rice

½ C. dry white wine

1 T. fresh basil, chopped (or 1 t. dried basil leaves)

¼ t. sea salt, to taste

1½–2 C. cooked chicken

¼ C. milk (2% or whole milk work best. Half and half is also fine, though higher in fat)

½ C. Parmesan cheese, shredded

In a saucepan, heat stock to simmering and cover until needed. If stock was refrigerated, skim fat prior to heating.

In a chef's pan or minimum 3-quart saucepan, melt butter over medium heat and sauté onion, garlic, and mushrooms until soft. Add rice and wine. Simmer, stirring constantly until wine is nearly evaporated. Season with basil and sea salt.

Add heated stock one cup at a time. With each cup, stir until liquid is absorbed. Continue to add stock until risotto has cooked 20 minutes, tasting to make sure it's fully cooked.

Stir in chicken, milk, and cheese. Heat thoroughly 2–3 minutes. Cover and remove from heat. Let rest 2–3 minutes prior to serving.

> I have trouble with toast. Toast is very difficult. You have to watch it all the time or it burns up.
>
> — *Julia Child*
>
> Source: quotegeek.com

Hungarian Chicken and Noodles Skillet Meal

Serve this dish over cooked egg noodles or combine noodles and sauce for a one skillet meal. Whichever method you choose, you're sure to love the result! Serves 4.

Prepare noodles al dente according to package directions. Be careful not to overcook.

Meanwhile, in a large non-stick skillet, heat oil over medium heat. Add onion and mushrooms and sauté 4–5 minutes until soft. Remove from skillet and set aside. In the same skillet, melt butter and whisk in flour to form a paste.

Add mustard and milk, whisking until smooth. Gradually add chicken stock, stirring frequently with whisk to bring mixture to a boil. Reduce heat and add salt, pepper and parsley.

Stir in reserved onion and mushroom mixture, plus sour cream, chicken and paprika. Simmer gently 2–4 minutes until chicken is thoroughly heated.

Add cooked egg noodles and toss together, or if preferred, simply serve over cooked egg noodles.

8 oz. uncooked egg noodles

2 T. extra virgin olive oil

1 C. yellow onion, chopped

2 C. (about 6 oz.) brown mushrooms, sliced

1½ T. butter

1½ T. all-purpose flour

1½ T. prepared coarse grain mustard

¼ C. evaporated milk (whole or low-fat)

1½ C. chicken stock (see page 14)

Sea salt, to taste

½ t. ground black pepper, to taste

2 T. fresh parsley, chopped (or 1 T. freeze-dried)

1 C. low-fat sour cream or plain yogurt

2 C. cooked chicken, cut bite size

½ t. paprika (freshly ground if available)

Chicken á la King

Many culinary historians credit the chef of Delmonico's, the famous New York restaurant, with developing Chicken à la King. Foxhall Keene, son of a Wall Street financier, supposedly suggested a pimiento-laden cream sauce. Over time, the name Chicken à la Keene evolved to Chicken à la King. Adding egg yolk is a classic preparation that adds velvety creaminess. Many thanks to Michéle Leroux Bustamante for contributing the basic recipe. Serves 4.

---

4 Pepperidge Farm® Frozen Puff Pastry Shells (or equivalent)

Chicken Mixture:

1 C. white onion, diced

½ C. green bell pepper, seeded and diced

¾ C. brown mushrooms, diced

3 T. butter

3 T. all-purpose flour

1¼ C. milk (2%, whole or soymilk)

½ C. chicken stock (see page 14)

2 large egg yolks, beaten

Sea salt and black pepper, to taste

2 T. pimiento, diced

¼ t. grated nutmeg, to taste

2 C. cooked chicken, cut to bite size

3 T. white wine, sherry, or dry vermouth

Shredded fresh Parmesan cheese to garnish

Pre-heat oven for pastry shells according to package directions.

In a 10" saucepan over medium heat, melt butter and sauté onion, pepper and mushrooms until onion is translucent and mushrooms have released juices and begun to cook down.

Add flour gradually, stirring thoroughly until smooth. Gradually add cold milk and chicken stock.

In a small bowl, separate egg yolks (whites may be covered and refrigerated up to 24 hours for later use). Stir approximately ½ C. sauce into yolks, and then add back into sauce mixture.

As mixture begins to simmer, add pimiento and season with salt, pepper and nutmeg. Reduce heat and continue to simmer an additional 10 minutes.

Meanwhile, bake frozen puff pastry shells according to package directions. Chicken is best when served on freshly baked pastry shells.

Add chicken and wine, and cook 5 more minutes, stirring frequently until chicken is thoroughly heated and shells are ready.

Remove pastry lids and pour chicken mixture into individual shells. Mixture should spill over sides of the pastry shell. Garnish with cheese and serve.

► *Cooking Tip: Chicken mixture should pour easily without being runny. Add additional milk if the mixture is too thick. If too thin, simmer uncovered until thickened.*

Chicken and Veggie Calzones

Aromatic and tangy, these calzones can be made with nearly any veggie and chicken combination. Try brown mushrooms, sun-dried tomatoes (cut, soak 10 minutes and drain), sliced black olives, whole garlic cloves, or zucchini. Serves 2–3.

Place sauce and a pinch of sugar in a small pan and simmer while preparing calzone and baking.

Combine all filling ingredients in a medium size bowl, stirring to distribute evenly. Set aside briefly, or cover and refrigerate until ready to use (it's fine to make the filling up to one day ahead, but add the cheese just before using).

To make two large single serving calzones with PPC: Slice dough in half then unroll, gently stretching each half to approximately 7″ × 9″. Place filling in the center of the dough leaving 2–3 inches at top and bottom and ¾″ at the right and left edges. Fold the upper and lower edges over the filling to create a seam at the top. Pinch to close top and side seams and bake as directed below (use a spatula or pizza paddle to transfer to oven).

If using traditional dough: Place dough on lightly floured surface (or use corn meal) and roll each piece to form a 10″–11″ circle. Place half of the filling in each circle, fold over and seal at edges to form the shape of a half moon.

Whichever crust you use, transfer to pizza stone (preferable) or lightly greased cookie sheet and bake at 400°F for 14–18 minutes or until golden brown.

Pour sauce over freshly baked calzones and garnish with Parmesan cheese just prior to serving.

Dough: **Pillsbury Pizza Crust® (PPC), or other prepared pizza dough**

12–14 oz. of your favorite marinara sauce

Pinch of sugar

Filling:

3 T. red onion, chopped

1 small red bell pepper, chopped

1¼ C. cooked chicken, bite size

1 T. fresh basil, chopped or 1 t. dried basil leaves

¼ t. red pepper flakes

½ C. shredded or grated Asiago cheese

¼ C. reduced-fat ricotta cheese

Salsa Chicken with Tortellini

A one-skillet meal that's ready in 20 minutes, this is a great meal to make when you don't want the "same old chicken". Readily available cheese tortellini is specified, but experiment with other kinds too. Serves 4.

1½ T. extra virgin olive oil

½ C. red onion, diced

1 medium zucchini, diced

1 medium red bell pepper, chopped

8-9 oz. frozen cheese tortellini

2 C. chicken meat, bite size

2 C. fresh chunky salsa (medium-hot)

In a 12" skillet or chef's pan over medium heat, heat oil and sauté onion, zucchini, and red pepper 2–3 minutes, or until vegetables begin to soften.

Add frozen tortellini and then add chicken. Do not stir. Distribute salsa evenly over chicken and pasta so that both are covered. Cover tightly and simmer 7–15 minutes or until tortellini is desired doneness.

▶ Cooking Tip: Tortellini may be refrigerated or frozen. When frozen, expect tortellini to take a few extra minutes. Choose the smallest size available.

Chicken is popular both at home and out on the town: Consumers purchase just over half of all chickens sold —54%— through grocery stores. Restaurants and other food service outlets account for 46%.

Source: eatchicken.com

Spanish Chicken with Wild Rice

You'll need to hurry to finish in 30 minutes, but clean-up is easy with only one skillet. Wild rice is recommended, but try any long-grain rice for a change of pace. Serves 4.

In a deep skillet (12") or a large chef's pan, heat the oil to medium heat and sauté bell peppers 2 minutes. Add the onion, garlic and ham, and continue to sauté another 2–3 minutes until onion is soft.

Add tomatoes, cayenne red pepper sauce, cilantro, chicken stock, and sea salt. Increase heat and bring to a boil.

Add rice, stir and cover tightly. Simmer over low heat 15–18 minutes until rice is nearly done (still a bit chewy). Stir in chicken and season with additional salt and black pepper. Cook an additional 3–5 minutes, stirring occasionally, until rice is fully cooked and chicken is heated through.

2 T. olive oil

1 medium red bell pepper, seeded and diced

½ medium green bell pepper, seeded and diced

1 medium white onion, diced

2–3 cloves garlic, minced

2 oz. smoked ham (½" cubes or bite size slices)

1 can (14 oz.) diced stewed tomatoes with Mexican seasonings

1 T. cayenne red pepper sauce

1 t. cilantro leaves, dried

2½ C. chicken stock, unsalted (see page 14)

¾ t. sea salt, to taste

1 C. long-grain wild rice

2 C. cooked chicken, shredded

½ t. black pepper, freshly ground

> Darkening of meat near bones occurs when the bones have not calcified completely because pigment from the bone marrow seeps through the porous bones. This is most common in young broiler-fryers although freezing can also contribute. When the chicken is cooked, the pigment turns dark, but the chicken is still perfectly safe to eat.
>
> Source: eatchicken.com

Fast, No-Bake Chicken Mornay

While assembling the recipes for this book, I found at least a dozen for Chicken Mornay, and was perplexed that no two were even similar. No wonder. Some research revealed that the word "mornay" can refer to any cheese-flavored cream sauce. It may have been named after Philippe de Mornay, a 15th century French Huguenot. This one is easy, creamy, and wonderfully delicious. Serves 4–5.

---

8 oz. wide egg noodles, cooked and drained

¼ C. chicken stock (see page 14) or 3 T. olive oil

1 T. butter

4 T. all-purpose flour

3 C. milk (2% or whole)

1 egg yolk (extra large)

3 T. white wine or dry vermouth

1 C. fresh Parmesan cheese, shredded

3 T. diced pimiento

2½ C. cooked chicken, cut to bite-size

Sea salt and black pepper, to taste

Cook egg noodles according to package directions. Drain and set aside until ready to use.

While the noodles cook, combine chicken stock and butter in a large saucepan over medium heat, and whisk in flour to form a paste. Add the milk gradually, one-half cup at a time, and continue stirring until mixture begins to thicken (about 5 minutes).

Remove approximately ½ C. sauce to a small bowl and beat the egg yolk into it before returning it to the skillet (this helps the egg stay cool and helps you avoid making scrambled eggs). Add wine (don't worry if a little extra spills into the skillet).

Stir in ½ C. Parmesan cheese, and add pimiento and chicken. Season with salt and pepper, to taste, and heat thoroughly.

Fold cooked noodles back into skillet, and cover for 2–3 minutes to reheat noodles. Transfer to a serving dish and sprinkle with remaining Parmesan. Serve hot.

Wine Pairing: A light Sauvignon Blanc or Pinot Grigio will complement the light texture of the white sauce. Open a bottle to make the sauce and finish it with dinner!

Your Chicken Is Cooked

Biscuits and Chicken Gravy

Rich gravy made from stock plus fresh biscuits highlight this hearty recipe. Great for a fast dinner! The open-faced sandwich version can be on the table in 10 minutes. Broccoli flowerets make a nice addition to the gravy, or simply steam them and serve as a side dish. Very tasty All-American fare. Serves 4.

Pre-heat oven to 400°F. Combine biscuit ingredients and mix thoroughly. Drop onto ungreased baking sheet and bake 10–12 minutes, or until light golden brown.

While biscuits are baking, in a large skillet or chef's pan, pre-heat olive oil and sauté onion 2–3 minutes over medium heat until soft. Add chicken stock and increase heat to bring stock to a simmer.

In a separate cup or bowl, whisk together flour and cold water or milk then gradually stir into stock mixture, stirring constantly. Add chicken, continuing to stir frequently, 4–5 minutes until thickened. Season with salt and pepper.

Variations: For more choices in old-fashioned comfort food, try the chicken gravy over waffles or as open faced hot chicken sandwiches.

To spice things up a bit, add ¼ t. red pepper flakes and 1 C. broccoli flowerets, bite size and steamed to 75% done. Add broccoli and red pepper flakes with chicken.

Drop Biscuits
(makes 4–5 biscuits)

1½ C. low-fat baking mix such as Bisquick®

½ C. low-fat milk (or soymilk)

Gravy

½ T. olive oil or butter

2 T. white or red onion, minced

2½ C. chicken stock (see page 14)

2½ T. all-purpose flour

½ C. cold water, milk, or evaporated milk (milk makes creamier gravy)

2 C. cooked chicken, shredded or thin-sliced

Sea salt, to taste

½ t. ground black pepper, to taste

Teriyaki Chicken and Pineapple over Basmati Rice

The pineapple plus the nutty quality of the Basmati rice take this dish to the tropics. Add a few toasted macadamia nut halves to land in paradise. Sweet onions (such as Vidalia or Walla Walla) are a great treat in this recipe. Serves 4.

2¼ C. unsalted chicken stock (see page 14)

½ t. sea salt

1 C. uncooked long grain basmati or jasmine rice

1½ T. macadamia nut oil (or canola)

1 C. sweet yellow onion, chopped

¾ C. prepared teriyaki sauce (preferably Hawaiian style)

1 C. fresh or frozen pineapple (bite size chunks with juice)

¼ C. macadamia nut pieces

2 C. cooked chicken

Place the chicken stock, sea salt, and rice in a 2-quart baking dish, and microwave uncovered on high (microwaves vary, estimate 10–11 minutes) until done. Rice should be flaky when tested with a fork and soft rather than crunchy.

While rice is cooking, heat oil in a 10" skillet, and sauté onion over medium heat until soft. Add teriyaki sauce, pineapple (frozen pineapple chunks need not be thawed), and macadamia nut pieces. Heat to simmer, stirring occasionally until all ingredients are thoroughly heated. Add chicken and continue to simmer 1–2 more minutes.

Gently layer teriyaki mixture on top of cooked rice, distributing evenly (try to do this step immediately after rice finishes). Cover and let mixture stand 5 minutes before serving.

Alternative preparation method: If you prefer to use a rice cooker or the stovetop to prepare rice, simply prepare the rice using chicken stock until fully cooked. Place rice in a serving dish and top with teriyaki mixture. Serve and enjoy.

Simmered Orange Chicken

As it simmers, this dish cooks down to create a rich, syrupy sauce that complements chicken perfectly. Serve over rice to enhance the oriental feel created by the ginger and sesame oil. Steamed broccoli could be added, or simply serve alongside a fresh green salad. Serves 3–4.

Begin by heating the chicken stock in a deep 10" skillet, chef's pan, or wok over medium-high heat.

Meanwhile, in a small bowl, whisk cornstarch into wine to dissolve. Continuing with a whisk, blend cornstarch mixture into chicken stock, and simmer 4–5 minutes to reduce slightly.

If serving over rice, prepare as directed on package and begin cooking rice during this first simmer.

Stir in orange juice, honey, and parsley, as well as ginger, salt and pepper.

Simmer briskly over medium heat for 15 minutes or until sauce thickens. Add sesame oil, taste, and adjust seasoning as needed.

Fold in chicken and heat thoroughly, 3–5 minutes.

Serve steaming hot over long grain white rice.

Wine pairing: Chardonnay

Variation: Add 1½ C. steamed broccoli flowerets along with chicken. Season broccoli with a pinch of salt prior to steaming.

¾ **C. chicken stock (see page 14)**

¼ **C. dry white wine (such as Chardonnay)**

2 **t. cornstarch**

¾ **C. orange juice (not from concentrate)**

2 **T. honey**

2 **T. fresh or freeze-dried parsley, chopped**

¼ **t. sea salt**

½ **t. ground black pepper**

½ **t. ground ginger**

1 **t. sesame oil**

2½ **C. cooked chicken, bite size**

1 **C. (uncooked) long grain white rice**

Chicken Pesto Linguini

Extremely easy and fast to prepare, here's a pasta dish that melts in your mouth. Buy extra rotisserie chicken to make sure you have enough 'leftovers' for this dish! Of course, many stores now offer very good prepared pesto sauce to make things even easier. Serves 6.

---

12 oz. linguini

3 large garlic cloves, chopped

3 C. fresh basil (do not substitute)

3 T. Parmesan cheese, grated (fresh)

2–3 T. pine nuts

1 C. extra virgin olive oil

Black pepper to taste

1½ T. additional olive oil

2 C. cooked chicken, bite size

Boil pasta in salt water according to package directions. Cook just to al dente (if using fresh pasta, make sauce first).

While pasta cooks, in a food processor, combine garlic, basil, cheese and pine nuts and process until finely chopped. With the machine running, add olive oil gradually, blending until all ingredients are well-incorporated.

Pre-heat a chef's pan or large skillet pre-heating 1½ T. olive oil to medium heat. Toss chicken in skillet to warm thoroughly. Add freshly made pesto sauce and pasta, tossing to coat pasta evenly. Continue to toss until heated and serve immediately.

Variation: Use the pesto sauce shown here along with a prepared crust to make Chicken Pesto Pizza.

The well-worn saying, "Don't count your chickens before they are hatched" originated as the moral of Aesop's fable, *The Milkmaid and Her Pail* in approximately 600 B.C.

More Main Dishes
Easy recipes that require a little more time

Chicken Cannelloni Florentine

Shredded chicken replaces beef and veal in this adaptation of an Italian classic. Any combination of cooked light and dark meat will do. Quick to make when using prepared marinara sauce, and extra filled pasta tubes freeze well for future use. Serves 6 (2 per person).

Sauce: use 1½ jars (26 oz. each) of your favorite prepared marinara sauce

or:

1 T. olive oil

1 C. white onion, finely chopped

2 cloves garlic, pressed and minced

2 T. red bell pepper, finely chopped

3 cans (14 oz. each) diced stewed tomatoes (Italian style)

3 T. tomato paste

⅛ t. sea salt, to taste

½ t. freeze-dried or fresh parsley

½ t. oregano leaves, dried (or 1½ t. fresh)

1 t. basil leaves, dried (or 1 T. fresh)

Filling:

2 C. (16 oz.) small curd cottage cheese

¾ package (10 oz.) chopped frozen spinach, thawed and drained

2½ C. cooked chicken, finely chopped or shredded

Sea salt and freshly ground black pepper to taste

1 t. cilantro leaves, dried

1 C. shredded Monterey Jack cheese

Pasta:

Package of at least 12 manicotti shells (2 per serving)

¼ C. fresh Parmesan cheese, shredded

Sauce: In a large saucepan or chef's pan, heat the oil over medium heat and sauté the onion, red bell pepper and garlic 4–5 minutes (until soft). Add tomatoes, tomato paste, sea salt and herbs. Increase heat and bring to a simmer. Reduce heat to continue simmering. Loosely cover and stir occasionally until ready to use.

Filling: Combine all filling ingredients in a large bowl and mix well.

Final Preparation: Preheat oven to 425°F. Spoon a thin layer of marinara sauce into the bottom of a 9" × 13" baking dish. Prepared sauce need not be heated. Stuff uncooked pasta tubes with filling (spoon it into the shells with an ice tea spoon) and arrange in a single layer in baking dish. Cover completely (don't leave pasta exposed) with remaining marinara sauce and garnish top with Parmesan cheese.

Cover loosely with foil (poke ventilation holes with fork). Bake 20 minutes at 425°F then reduce oven temperature to 375°F. Bake 30 minutes more or until pasta shells test done.

With any extra filling, fill additional tubes and place in freezer bag. Defrost within a few weeks and finish as above.

Your Chicken Is Cooked

Chicken Stuffed Bell Peppers

Use any combination of light and dark meat in this tangy, fresh-tasting dish. Quick to make though longer to bake, this easy recipe is a winner. Try yellow bell peppers for a sweeter variation. Makes 6 peppers.

6 medium red bell peppers
Sauce: use your favorite prepared marinara sauce*
or:
1 T. olive oil
1 C. white onion, finely chopped
2 cloves garlic, peeled and minced
3 T. red bell pepper
1 can (28 oz.) diced stewed tomatoes (Italian style)
2 T. tomato paste
½ t. cilantro leaves, dried
½ t. oregano leaves, dried (or 1½ t. fresh)
1 t. basil leaves, dried (or 1 T. fresh)
Sea salt, to taste

Filling:
½ C. cooked long grain jasmine, basmati or white rice
1 C. fresh baby spinach leaves, chopped
2 C. cooked chicken
1 C. marinara sauce from above
2 t. cayenne red pepper sauce, to taste
¼ C. chicken stock (see page 14)
¼ C. small curd cottage cheese (low-fat)
1 t. cilantro leaves, dried
½ C. shredded mozzarella cheese (or similar favorite)

Garnish: 6 slices mozzarella, sliced ⅛" thick

*Use a prepared sauce with sweet bell peppers or garden vegetables.

Bell peppers: Choose well-proportioned peppers that will remain upright when stuffed. Wash and core to remove seeds and stem.

In a hurry sauce: It is not necessary to heat sauce prior to baking. Proceed to make the filling.

Sauce (slow version): Using a large saucepan or chef's pan, heat the oil to medium heat and sauté the onion, red bell pepper and garlic cloves 2–3 minutes (until soft). Add tomatoes, tomato paste, sea salt and herbs. Increase heat and bring to a simmer. Reduce heat and continue simmering. Loosely cover and stir occasionally for at least one hour until ready to use.

Filling: Combine all filling ingredients in a large bowl and mix well.

Preheat oven to 425°F. Stuff bell peppers with filling mix and place in baking dish. Pour remaining marinara sauce around peppers. Cover loosely with foil. Bake 40 minutes at 425°F Remove briefly from oven and reduce temperature to 350°F.

Top peppers with garnish of cheese. Bake 10–12 minutes more uncovered (or until cheese is slightly brown).

Chicken and Eggplant Parmesan en Casserole

Shredded chicken enhances the flavor of this adaptation of an Italian classic. The extra step of browning the eggplant takes a bit of time, but helps get the moisture out of the eggplant. Test kitchen preparation took just over 35 minutes using prepared sauce, plus 50 minutes of baking. Prepare the casserole up to 2 days prior to baking and enjoy! Makes 4 generous servings.

Sauce: use 1½ jars (26 oz. each) of your favorite prepared marinara sauce or use the sauce recipe on page 100

Eggplant: 2 medium eggplants, peeled and cut into ¼"– ½" slices*

1–2 eggs, beaten

½ C. whole wheat or all-purpose flour

½ T. sea salt

½ t. fresh ground black pepper

¾ C. white onion, finely chopped

3 large cloves garlic, peeled and minced

*Buy eggplant that is long and narrow (similar in appearance to zucchini). Remove seeds if using larger eggplant.

Sauce: If using a prepared sauce, simply pour straight from the jar. We tested with Barilla® sauces (Garden Vegetable and Sweet Bell Pepper).

Eggplant: In a large skillet, heat the oil to medium and sauté the onion and garlic 2–3 minutes until soft. Reserve onions and garlic for use in casserole (See below).

Dip eggplant pieces in beaten egg. Combine with flour, salt and pepper in a bag and shake to coat. Add coated eggplant pieces to skillet in a single layer and brown 4–5 minutes per side.

Brown half the eggplant, remove to paper towels to drain and add remaining coated eggplant to skillet. Assemble casserole while browning remaining eggplant.

Chicken and Eggplant Parmesan en Casserole

(continued)

Casserole: Preheat oven to 425°F. Spoon sauce to coat bottom of an 8" square baking dish. Distribute sautéed onion and garlic evenly and top with a layer of eggplant. Continue with one layer each of chicken, sauce, ricotta, spinach, and cheese. Also add cilantro.

Add another layer of eggplant then a final layer of marinara sauce. To prevent drying, don't leave exposed chicken or eggplant. Garnish top with Parmesan.

Cover loosely with foil (poke ventilation holes with fork). Bake 30 minutes at 425°F then reduce temperature to 350°F. Bake 20–30 minutes more or until sauce is well-heated and bubbly.

Casserole: Eggplant and sauce from p. 102, plus:

½ **C. ricotta cheese or small curd cottage cheese**

¾ **C. chopped baby spinach (or ½ package frozen)**

1½ **C. cooked chicken, bite-size or shredded**

½ **t. cilantro leaves, dried (optional)**

¾ **C. shredded mozzarella cheese (or similar favorite)**

¼ **C. fresh Parmesan cheese to garnish**

> U.S. consumers eat more chicken per person than people of any other country in the world. In the U.S., chicken represents 35% of all meat consumed.
>
> Which regions eat the most chicken per capita? Chicken used to be most popular in the South, but as of 2001, the Northeast is the leading region (still followed closely by the South).
>
> Source: USDA Economic Research

Low-fat, Extremely Tasty Chicken Lasagna

Made with low-fat cottage cheese rather than ricotta and chicken rather than beef, here's a lasagna that sacrifices nothing in taste. This easy recipe is a great crowd pleaser. A deep loaf pan that can accommodate at least three layers is ideal, or make two small pans and freeze one! Serves 6–8.

---

1 package no-bake lasagna noodles or fresh noodles*

In a hurry sauce:

2 jars (26 oz. each) marinara sauce

½ t. sugar per jar

For days when you have more time, make sauce as follows:

1 T. olive oil

1 small white onion, finely chopped

1 C. brown or baby Portobello mushrooms, sliced (4–5 oz.)

3 cloves garlic, peeled (minced)

¼ C. red bell pepper, finely chopped

4 cans (14 oz. each) diced stewed tomatoes (preferably Italian style)

3 T. tomato paste

Sauce (in a hurry version): No heating required. Simply stir in the sugar and proceed to Final Preparation below.

Sauce (slow version): Using a 3-quart saucepan or chef's pan, heat the oil to medium heat and sauté the onion, garlic, red bell pepper, and mushrooms 3–5 minutes (until soft). Add tomatoes, tomato paste, sea salt, sugar and spices. Increase heat and bring to a simmer. Add chicken and adjust heat to continue simmering. Loosely cover and stir occasionally until ready to use.

Final Preparation (both versions): Preheat oven to 425°F. Place a few spoonfuls of sauce in bottom of baking dish to coat bottom. Begin layering noodles (uncooked), sauce, cottage cheese, spinach, mushrooms, chicken (if not already in sauce) and shredded cheese to create the lasagna. Be careful to distribute ingredients evenly, including corners. Frozen spinach need not be thawed if it can be separated. Otherwise, thaw in microwave.

Low-fat, Extremely Tasty
Chicken Lasagna

(continued)

At final layer, top only with sauce (leave no pasta exposed) and garnish with shredded Parmesan. Reserve some sauce, if desired, to spoon over lasagna when serving. Cover loosely with foil. Bake 30 minutes at 425°F then reduce oven temperature to 375°F. Bake 20–30 minutes more, or until lasagna is thoroughly heated and bubbly.

Remove pan from oven and let stand at least 10–15 minutes prior to slicing to help keep lasagna layers intact when serving. Spoon reserved sauce over lasagna pieces, if desired.

*Any lasagna noodles will work fine. "No Bake" noodles are a bit thinner and lighter, but are not a requirement.

> LOVE: A word properly applied to our delight in particular kinds of food; sometimes metaphorically spoken of the favorite objects of all our appetites.
>
> — *Henry Fielding*
>
> Source: quotationspage.com

Sea salt, to taste

Black pepper, to taste

½ t. sugar

1 t. cilantro leaves, dried or parsley flakes

1 t. oregano leaves, dried (or 1 T. fresh, minced)

1½ t. basil leaves, dried (or 1½ T. fresh, chopped)

Lasagna layers:

14 oz. small curd cottage cheese (low-fat works best)

2 C. cooked chicken, diced or shredded

2 C. shredded mozzarella cheese (or similar favorite), shredded

1 C. fresh or frozen chopped spinach

¾ C. brown mushrooms, sliced or chopped (uncooked)

¼ C. Parmesan cheese (top layer only)

Florentine Chicken Casserole

This easy, all-in-one serving dish meal takes about 20–25 minutes to prepare plus another 25 to bake. It's scrumptious over white rice. Serves 4.

---

1 package (10 oz.) frozen chopped spinach

2 T. butter, divided

1 clove garlic, crushed and minced

¼ C. white onion, minced

½ t. dried basil

½ t. dried thyme

2 T. all-purpose flour, divided

½ C. whole milk

2½ C. cooked chicken, sliced or torn

½ C. half-and-half

½ C. chicken stock (see page 14)

Sea salt and black pepper, to taste

6 thin slices ham (about ¼ lb.)

1 C. fresh Parmesan cheese, shredded

Thaw spinach, drain well, and set aside.

Meanwhile, in a large skillet over medium heat, melt 1 T. butter, and add minced garlic, onion, basil, and thyme. Reduce heat to medium-low and cook, stirring constantly, for 2–3 minutes until onion is translucent. Add 1 T. flour and blend well.

Add milk and spinach. Gently simmer, stirring constantly, for 5 minutes. Place spinach mixture into a lightly buttered 2-quart casserole or baking dish.

In the same skillet over medium-low heat, melt remaining butter and blend in remaining 1 T. flour. Gradually add half-and-half and chicken stock, stirring frequently until slightly thickened. Add ¼ C. of cheese and season with sea salt and pepper. While sauce thickens, layer chicken and ham over spinach in baking dish.

Pour sauce over chicken and ham, and top with remaining Parmesan cheese. Bake uncovered 25 minutes at 375°F, or until casserole is lightly browned and bubbly. Serve immediately.

Arroz con Pollo (Rice with Chicken)

This dish traces its roots to both Mexico and Spain. Thanks to Keith Fisher for contributing this traditional recipe. Serves 4.

In a large, deep skillet over medium-high heat, sauté the onion, pepper, garlic, tomato, saffron, and cilantro in olive oil until vegetables are soft.

Add in chicken, tomato sauce, and salt, continuing over medium-high heat until sauce is simmering and chicken is thoroughly heated.

Increase heat to high, and add water, chicken stock and rice, stirring occasionally until mixture comes to a simmer.

Cover pot with a snug-fitting lid, reduce heat to low, and allow mixture to steam/cook for 45 minutes.

After 45 minutes, fluff rice with a fork. If mixture is completely dry, add an additional ¼ C. water or chicken stock. Re-cover and cook for an additional 15 minutes. Test rice for doneness and serve.

Variation: Include 1 can (11 oz.) of either garbanzo beans or red kidney beans, drained and rinsed – add along with chicken.

3 T. olive oil

½ C. white or yellow onion, finely chopped

½ C. green pepper, finely chopped

4–6 cloves fresh garlic, finely chopped

1 Roma tomato, chopped

1 t. saffron or turmeric (optional)

8–10 sprigs fresh cilantro, finely chopped (or one T. dried)

2 C. cooked chicken, cut to 1"–2" pieces

¼ C. tomato sauce

Sea salt, to taste

2 C. water

2 C. chicken stock (see page 14)

2 C. long grain white rice

Chicken, Mushroom and Rice Casserole

Make this "leftovers" casserole with canned cream of chicken soup, or use leftovers of Modern Cream of Mushroom soup in this book. Either way, this easy meal tastes great. Serves 4.

---

1 C. long grain rice, uncooked (try basmati or jasmine)

2 C. chicken stock (see page 14)

1½ T. olive oil

¾ C. white onion, chopped (1 small onion)

1 clove garlic, minced

1¼ C. brown mushrooms, thinly sliced or chopped

2 C. cooked chicken

Either:

1 can (10½ oz.) condensed Cream of Chicken soup, plus

1 C. milk (2%, whole, or soymilk)

or:

2 C. Cream of Chicken and Mushroom soup from page 27

Sea salt, to taste

¼ t. freshly ground black pepper, to taste

½ C. Parmesan cheese

Prepare rice using chicken stock (or water) according to package directions. Cook until just tender.

While rice is cooking: Pre-heat oven to 375°F. In a large skillet or chef's pan, heat the oil to medium and sauté the onion, garlic, and mushrooms 3–5 minutes (until soft).

Combine skillet ingredients with rice and soup ingredients in a deep 2-quart casserole. Mix thoroughly. Add salt and pepper, to taste. Mixture should be very moist. Add a bit of milk if necessary. Top with Parmesan cheese, cover and bake 20 minutes or until thoroughly heated and bubbly.

> …even regular supermarket chickens in the United States are on the whole excellent buys for the price, and although people often say that chickens don't taste as good as they used to, I believe ordinary supermarket chickens are better today. Thanks to improvements from cross-breeding, the meat is more moist and tender than it has ever been. When I was a teenage apprentice, the chicken had to be constantly basted and rested upside down after roasting in order to keep the breast moist, but today it is almost impossible to dry out the breast.
>
> — *Jacques Pépin*
>
> Source: Julia and Jacques Cooking at Home
> Julia Child and Jacques Pépin, (2000)

Down Home Chicken and Green Bean Skillet Meal

This recipe has "Americana" written all over it! Hopefully, your grandma made meals this good. Be sure to monitor carefully so that beans don't overcook. Serves 4.

In a chef's pan or deep skillet, heat the oil over medium heat and sauté the onion, garlic, and mushrooms 3–4 minutes (until soft). Sprinkle with flour and stir well to combine. Add chicken stock plus Dijon and continue to cook 1–2 minutes until heated, stirring often.

Add soup and mix thoroughly, followed by cooked noodles, green beans and chicken. Add seasonings to taste. Mixture should be very moist. Add additional chicken stock or water if necessary. Reduce heat to a gentle simmer, cover and cook 5–7 minutes or to desired crispness of beans.

Remove to serving dish or plates and top with Parmesan cheese. Serve promptly.

1½ T. olive oil

2 cloves garlic, pressed and minced

¼ C. white onion, chopped

¾ C. brown mushrooms, thinly sliced or chopped

1½ T. all-purpose flour

¾ C. chicken stock (see page 14)

2 t. Dijon mustard

Either:

½ can (10½ oz.) condensed Cream of Chicken soup, plus

¾ C. milk (2%, whole or soymilk)

Or:

1½ C. Modern Cream of Mushroom soup (page 27)

2 C. cooked egg noodles

1 C. frozen French cut green beans (or use fresh)

1 C. cooked chicken

Sea salt and freshly ground black pepper, to taste

¼ C. Parmesan cheese to garnish

Chicken consumption is up. In fact, it's way up! Americans consumed an average 28 pounds of chicken per person in 1960, increasing to about 81 pounds in 2002. Men and women ages 18 to 24 consume the most, and chicken is the number one animal species consumed in the United States. The 40-year trend of Americans eating more chicken and less beef is expected to continue for at least several more years. By the way, in real dollars (adjusted for inflation), chicken costs less today than it did 30 years ago.

Source: USDA Economic Research, courtesy of eatchicken.com

All-American Jumbo Chicken Pot Pie

Most of us are used to single-serving pot pies, but this full-size pie feeds an entire family. Easy and delicious, this pie takes 20–30 minutes using a prepared crust and 30–35 minutes to bake. Serves 6.

---

2 T. extra virgin olive oil

¾ C. white onion, chopped

1 C. brown mushrooms, sliced (2–3 oz.)

2 T. all-purpose flour

2 C. chicken stock (see page 14)

1 small zucchini, diced

1 large red potato, diced (no larger than ½" cubes)

1 medium tomato, diced

½ C. frozen petite peas

2½ C. cooked chicken, bite-size

¼ C. fresh Parmesan cheese, shredded

Sea salt and black pepper, to taste

½ t. cilantro, dried

Refrigerated pie crust for 2-crust pie

Preheat oven to 400°F. Set pie crust out of refrigerator (use at room temperature).

Heat olive oil over medium heat in a 3-quart or larger chef's pan or saucepan and sauté onion and mushroom until soft. Sprinkle flour over mushrooms and stir well to incorporate.

Gradually add chicken stock, continuing to stir often as mixture thickens and comes to a boil. Add zucchini, potato, tomato, and peas, simmering an additional 3–5 minutes, stirring frequently. Add chicken, cheese and seasonings, reduce heat to warm and cover until ready to use. Filling will continue to thicken as it rests.

Piecrust: Unfold bottom crust and center on a 9" pie plate.

Transfer heated pie filling to pie shell. Unfold top crust and center over filled shell. Avoid the temptation to over-fill. Chicken mixture should be level with top of pie plate, not heaped. Seal crust well by fluting edges and vent top well.

Place pie on a baking sheet and bake in center of oven until crust is deep golden brown and filling is thoroughly cooked (approx. 30–35 minutes). For easier serving, let pie "rest" for 10 minutes after baking. Slice as with a dessert pie and serve hot.

Classy, Creamy Florentine
Chicken Pot Pie

This pie provides comfort food for a family dinner yet it's classy enough to impress your friends. This dish not only looks and tastes great, it smells divine! Try the broccoli variation noted for a change of pace. Hint: If needed, place a foil collar over crust edges to avoid over-browning. Serves 6.

Preheat oven to 400°F. Set pie crust out of refrigerator (use at room temperature). Heat olive oil over medium heat in a 3-quart or larger chef's pan or saucepan and sauté onion and mushroom until soft, 3–4 minutes.

Sprinkle flour over mushrooms and stir well to incorporate. Gradually add chicken stock, continuing to stir often as mixture thickens and comes to a boil.

Reduce heat and add evaporated milk. Bring to a simmer then stir in spinach, seasoning, cheese, and chicken. Reduce heat to warm and cover until ready to use. Filling will thicken as it rests.

Piecrust: Unfold bottom crust and center on a 9" pie plate.

Add additional milk, if necessary, to make filling very moist but not runny, and transfer heated filling to pie shell. To avoid overflowing during baking, fill only until level with top of pie plate. Cover with top crust. Seal and flute edges and vent top well (Cut out half moons or other designs).

Bake until crust is golden brown and filling is thoroughly heated (approx. 30–35 minutes). Let pie "rest" for 10 minutes prior to serving.

2 T. olive oil

1 medium white onion, finely chopped (1 C.)

1 C. brown mushrooms, sliced (2–3 oz.)

2 T. all-purpose flour

1½ C. chicken stock (see page 14)

½ C. evaporated milk

1½ C. chopped spinach, thawed and drained

¼ t. sea salt, to taste

½ t. freshly ground black pepper

½ C. fresh Parmesan cheese, shredded

½ C. mild Swiss cheese, grated (or other white cheese)

2½–3 C. cooked chicken

Refrigerated pie crust for 2-crust pie

Black Olive Chicken with Garlic and Basil

Olive lovers will be salivating when you make this flavorful Mediterranean dish. Serve over pasta or rice. Preparation time is 35 minutes. In keeping with the Mediterranean feel of this dish, serve over a bed of couscous (tiny pasta). Serves 4.

2 T. olive oil

1 small white onion, finely chopped

10 large garlic cloves, peeled (8 whole, 2 halved)

1 t. rosemary, dried (or 1 T. fresh)

½ C. dry white wine

1 can (28 oz.) diced stewed tomatoes (Italian style)

1 small can (6 oz.) tomato paste

½ C. chicken stock (see page 14)

½ C. black olives, chopped

Sea salt, to taste

3 T. fresh basil, finely chopped (1 T. dried basil leaves)

2 ½ C. cooked chicken (leave some larger white meat strips)

Using a deep skillet (12") or a large saucepan or chef's pan, heat the oil over medium heat and sauté the onion and garlic cloves 2–3 minutes until soft. Add the rosemary and white wine, stirring often, and simmer 3–4 minutes until wine is noticeably reduced.

Add tomatoes, tomato paste, chicken stock, olives, and seasonings. Increase heat and simmer for 15 minutes. Add chicken and reduce heat to low, stirring occasionally.

Cook uncovered an additional 7–10 minutes, stirring occasionally, until sauce is thickened and chicken is heated through.

Cook couscous or other pasta, if desired, and place in serving plates or bowls. Top with chicken and enjoy!

> Reminds me of my safari in Africa. Somebody forgot the corkscrew and for several days we had to live on nothing but food and water.
>
> — W. C. Fields
>
> Source: quotationspage.com

Chicken and Dressing Casserole

Although I usually avoid canned soups and prepared foods, this is a good one for unexpected guests or an easy, kid-pleasing meal. Allow about 20–25 minutes preparation time, plus 35 minutes to bake. Serves 8.

Cut or tear chicken meat into bite-size pieces. In a very large mixing bowl, stir together soups, stock, chicken, and peas and pearl onions.

To reduce dirty dishes, use the casserole you intend to bake in to combine the stuffing mix (we tested with Mrs. Cubbison's®), butter, and apple butter. Add dressing to chicken mixture, stirring well.

Spray one 5-quart or two smaller casserole dishes with cooking spray or grease with butter or oil. Return the combined mixture to the casserole dish(es), and top with shredded cheese.

Cover and bake 35 minutes at 375°F or until thoroughly heated. Remove cover for the final 5–10 minutes to aid browning, if desired.

4 C. cooked chicken

1 can (10 oz.) cream of mushroom soup, undiluted

1 can (10 oz.) cream of celery soup, undiluted

2 C. chicken stock (see page 14)

8 oz. frozen petite peas and pearl onions

1 package, herb-seasoned cube stuffing (10 oz.)

¼ C. butter, melted

¼ C. apple butter

½ C. shredded cheese (try a blend of pizza-type cheeses)

According to the National Chicken Council, skinless, boneless breast is the chicken product purchased most often for cooking at home.

Source: eatchicken.com

Traditional Tomato Sauce Pizza

Making your own pizza is much more economical and can be just as fast as pizza delivery. These days, prepared crusts are easy to find, and some even include the sauce! Makes 4 individual pizzas.

Crust:
4 prepared crusts, 7"

Sauce:
1½ C. prepared marinara sauce

2 large garlic cloves, minced

2–3 Roma tomatoes, minced

1 T. fresh basil (or 1 t. dried)

½ t. sugar

Toppings:
1½ C. cooked chicken

2 C. mozzarella or Italian cheeses

¾ C. Parmesan cheese, grated (fresh)

Fresh bell pepper, any color

Sun-dried tomatoes, 1 oz. (soak 10 min., drain and chop)

Zucchini or other squash, chopped

Bell pepper (red, yellow, or orange)

Pre-heat oven to 450°F, also pre-heating pizza stone on center rack.

Crust: Use your favorite pre-prepared crust.

Sauce: Combine sauce ingredients in a mixing bowl and stir well. Spoon sauce onto prepared pizza crusts.

Toppings: Chop desired toppings and distribute evenly on top of sauce.

Top pizzas with cheese and bake two at a time on pizza stone, 12–15 minutes or until cheese is lightly browned.

Cut in half or quarters with pizza cutter or fold over and enjoy!

Variations: Mix and match toppings and crust types. Suggestions include artichoke hearts, 3–5 oz. cooked spicy sausage (sauté and drain well), chopped Roma tomatoes, freshly chopped basil or spinach.

> The trouble with eating Italian food is that five or six days later you're hungry again.
>
> — *George Miller*
>
> Source: quotationspage.com

Your Chicken Is Cooked

Chicken and Asparagus Casserole

Simple yet tasty, this casserole goes together quickly and bakes in about 40 minutes. No need to cook the noodles in advance. Serves 4.

Preheat oven to 400°F. In an ungreased 2-quart baking dish, combine all ingredients except Parmesan and stir thoroughly. If asparagus are frozen, thaw just enough to cut. Noodles should be submerged in liquid to cook properly.

Top with Parmesan and loosely cover baking dish with a glass cover or foil. Bake 20 minutes.

Reduce oven temperature to 350°F. Bake 30 minutes more or until noodles test done.

Note: If asparagus were frozen, increase baking time at 400°F to 25–30 minutes.

Butter or vegetable oil spray to coat baking dish

3 C. chicken stock (see page 14)

1 C. white onion, chopped

8 oz. (uncooked) thin egg noodles

2 C. cooked chicken, shredded

1 C. fresh or frozen asparagus, cut bite size

¼ t. sea salt

½ t. ground black pepper, to taste

1 C. Monterey Jack cheese

½ C. shredded Parmesan cheese

> Food first, then morality.
>
> — *Bertolt Brecht "What Keeps Mankind Alive?"*
> *Act 2, sc. 6, Threepenny Opera*
>
> Source: The Columbia World of Quotations, 1996

Scalloped Potato and Chicken Casserole

Earthy and comforting, serve this casserole on a cool or rainy day with a side of bright green vegetables. *Tip:* It's important to use a deep baking dish. Serves 6.

3–4 large potatoes (peeled and thinly sliced)

½ large sweet onion, very thinly sliced

2 C. cooked chicken, shredded

1 C. Monterey Jack cheese, shredded

2½–4 C. hot low-fat milk (depending on depth of casserole)

Sea salt and ground black pepper, to taste

3–4 T. butter or margarine

Pre-heat oven to 350°F. Grease a deep, oven-safe baking dish. Arrange a layer of potatoes to cover bottom of dish and top with a layer of sweet onion (use all onion in this layer). Add chicken meat and cheese, then dot with 1–2 T. butter.

Sprinkle with sea salt and pepper. Add another layer of potatoes and again dot with butter and sprinkle salt and pepper. Leave at least 1″ of space between top of potatoes and top of baking dish. Add hot milk to cover potatoes leaving at least ¾″ at top to allow milk to bubble without overflowing. Potatoes should be nearly submerged.

Bake uncovered for 1¼ hours, or until potatoes are lightly browned and tender.

> The term, "Chicken Pox" didn't derive from people who believed that it came from chickens; it came from the Old English term "gican pox" — which means, "the itching pox."
>
> Source: greenapple.com

Light Chicken Tetrazzini

Chicken Tetrazzini commemorates Luisa Tetrazzini (1874-1940), a well-known, well-fed soprano. The dish was extremely popular around the turn of the 20th century. Traditional tetrazzini is heavy on butter and cream. This lighter version tastes absolutely fabulous without a lot of the extra fat. Use real butter for best taste. Serves 4.

In a chef's pan or 3-quart saucepan, melt butter over medium heat and sauté garlic and mushrooms until soft, 3–4 minutes. Sprinkle flour lightly and stir briskly. Add white wine, then gradually stir in milk one-half cup at a time, stirring often as mixture heats and thickens.

Cook pasta in salted water according to package directions until al dente. Rinse with cool tap water to stop cooking process if not using immediately.

Meanwhile, heat sauce mixture to a gentle simmer, but do not boil. In a small bowl, whisk egg yolk together with a small amount of milk or white sauce. Stir into sauce mixture. Add sea salt and pepper to taste. Stir in chicken, cheese and spaghetti, mixing thoroughly.

Preheat broiler. Place spaghetti mixture in an 8" × 8" baking dish and top with bread crumbs. Place under broiler 4–6 minutes until lightly browned. Monitor carefully. Serve immediately.

3 T. butter

2 cloves garlic, minced

¾ C. Italian brown mushrooms, sliced

1½ T. flour (all purpose)

3 T. dry white wine or vermouth

2 C. milk (2%, whole milk or soymilk)

8 oz. thin spaghetti (vermicelli)

1 egg yolk

2 C. cooked chicken

Sea salt, to taste

White pepper, to taste

½ C. Parmesan cheese

2–3 T. Italian style bread crumbs

Chicken with Orzo and Yellow Peppers Gratin

This lovely casserole is very satisfying alongside a fresh green salad or a medley of colorful steamed vegetables. One of your author's favorites! Serves 4.

1+ C. chicken stock plus water to cook pasta (see page 14)

1 C. orzo (uncooked)

½ C. dry white wine

¾ C. chicken stock (see page 14)

2 cloves garlic, minced

2 C. yellow bell peppers, chopped

¼ C. milk (any type)

½ C. green onions, minced (include dark green tops)

1 C. pepper jack cheese, shredded*

½ t. red pepper flakes

2 C. chicken meat

1 large tomato, seeded and chopped (1 C.)

Sea salt, to taste

Freshly ground white or black pepper, to taste

¼ C. fresh Parmesan cheese, shredded

In a large saucepan bring 1 quart of salted water (including at least 1 C. chicken stock) to a boil and cook orzo, al dente. Drain and set aside.

In a separate skillet, simmer garlic and bell peppers in wine and stock, 12–15 minutes until very tender. Transfer to a food processor or blender and purée with milk. Pour puréed pepper mixture into saucepan with cooked orzo.

Preheat oven to 350°F.

Remove from heat and add green onions, pepper jack cheese, red pepper flakes and chicken. Gently fold in tomatoes and season with sea salt and pepper to taste.

Transfer mixture into a 2-quart casserole. Smooth top and garnish with Parmesan. Cover with a glass lid or foil.

Casserole may be prepared up to 24 hours ahead and refrigerated, covered.

Bake gratin in middle of oven 30 minutes (45 minutes if previously refrigerated). Gratin should be set and lightly browned. Remove cover for final 10 minutes of baking to aid browning.

*This dish can get spicy! For a milder version, substitute Mexican blend cheese or Monterey Jack and/or reduce red pepper flakes.

Chicken and Angel Hair Pasta with Onion Sauce

The flavor of the onions gets milder and sweeter as this dish cooks. Using white wine aged in oak adds a very subtle oak aftertaste. Serves 4–5.

Sauce: In a 4-quart chef's pan or deep skillet over medium heat, melt butter and sauté garlic and mushrooms 3–5 minutes until softened. Add wine and onions.

Cook at lowest heat (the intent is to sweat the onions, not brown them), covered, 30 minutes. Onions should soften and begin to caramelize.

Increase heat to medium-high, and then add stock, carrots, and herbs, bringing mixture to a boil. Reduce heat, cover and simmer an additional 20–30 minutes, stirring occasionally. Add water or additional stock as needed to keep ingredients very moist. The longer the onion cooks, the more mellow the taste.

Stir in chicken and cover, continuing to heat 4–6 minutes until chicken is thoroughly heated. Add sea salt to taste.

Final Preparation: In a 4-quart saucepan, bring 3 quarts of salted water to a boil and cook pasta, al dente.

Add pasta to onion mixture and toss. Garnish with parsley flakes. Serve immediately.

3 T. butter (or 1½ T. each olive oil and butter)

3 large garlic cloves, minced

1 C. brown mushrooms, sliced

½ C. dry white wine

3 large yellow onions, chopped

3½ C. chicken stock (see page 14)

6–8 baby carrots, quartered

1 t. dried basil (or 1 T. fresh)

½ t. thyme, dried (or 1½ t. fresh)

2½ C. cooked chicken

Sea salt, to taste

10–12 oz. angel hair pasta (or substitute thin spaghetti)

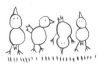

Chicken Cordon Bleu Casserole

When I first read recipes including crushed potato chips as a topping, I thought the authors were nuts (the cookbook I was reading was from the early 1960s). Then I tried it and I was hooked. Since then, I notice even Emeril uses potato chips to top casseroles. This yummy variety combines ham, chicken and cheeses to create a fabulous layered casserole with the flavors of Chicken Cordon Bleu. Serves 4–5.

1 C. thin egg noodles or ¾ C. orzo, uncooked

5 oz. Black Forest ham pieces (½" cubes or small slices)

1½ C. cooked chicken, bite size (preferably breast meat)

½ C. green onion, minced (include some dark green tops)

¼ t. freshly ground black pepper

½ C. white wine

1 C. milk (preferably whole milk)

1 C. chicken stock (see page 14)

1¼ C. Swiss or similar white cheese, shredded

3 oz. crushed potato chips*

Preheat oven to 425°F with rack in center of oven.

In a deep 2-quart baking dish, start with a layer of pasta. Next layer ham pieces, chicken and green onions. Add ground black pepper to season.

Distribute white wine, milk and chicken stock evenly. Top with a layer of cheese followed by the crumbled potato chips.

Bake 20–25 minutes (uncovered) or until golden brown and bubbly. Reduce oven temperature to 350°F, and bake an additional 20 minutes. Cover loosely if casserole browns too much.

Taste to make sure pasta is fully cooked. Let casserole rest 5 minutes prior to serving.

*Try plain, salt & vinegar, or ranch flavor chips. If chips are unsalted, add a sprinkle of salt prior to baking.

Spaghetti with Chicken and Red Pepper Sauce

A delicious alternative to traditional tomato sauce, this red pepper sauce has a unique smoky, mellow taste. Serve over almost any type of pasta. Serves 2.

Lightly char the peppers (whole) in a broiler/toaster oven or conventional oven at 375°F for 20 minutes, turning every 5 minutes to char all sides. Remove and plunge into ice water to shrivel the peppers. Peel off skins, seed, and coarsely chop.

In a large skillet (while the peppers roast), heat olive oil and slowly sauté onion and garlic until onion is translucent (12–15 minutes). Also heat salted water to cook spaghetti.

Place onion mixture in either a food processor or blender (leave the skillet out for the next step), and process for a few seconds. Add the peppers, lemon juice, chicken stock, milk, and seasonings and purée, leaving sauce chunky. Thin with additional milk, if necessary.

Add pasta to salted water, and cook al dente, per package directions.

In the skillet used for the onion, pre-heat olive oil and add chicken. Heat 1 minute over medium heat then return sauce to skillet and add cooked pasta. Toss to coat. Serve immediately.

3 medium red bell peppers

2 T. olive oil (or 1 T. each, olive oil and butter)

1 medium red onion

2–3 cloves garlic

1 T. lemon juice

½ C. chicken stock or water

¼ C. 2%, whole milk, evaporated milk or soymilk

Sea salt and freshly ground black pepper, to taste

1½ t. basil leaves, dried (or 1½ T. fresh, chopped)

1–1½ C. cooked chicken, bite size

4 oz. thin spaghetti (or other pasta)

Chicken Enchilada Casserole

Sort of a "Southwestern Lasagna," this layered casserole is delicious with cornbread and black or refried beans. A fresher tasting version of traditional south-of-the-border fare, use a mild salsa to reduce the spiciness. Serves 4.

1 can (14 oz.) mild enchilada sauce (red)

1½ C. fresh chunky salsa (medium-hot)

1 T. lime juice

1 can (4 oz.) diced green chilies (mild)

3 C. cooked chicken, diced

1 t. ground cumin

2 C. Monterey Jack or Mexican blend cheese, shredded

4–6 medium (7"–8") corn tortillas

Low-fat sour cream and guacamole

Optional Ingredient:

¼ C. almonds, slivered or shaved

Pre-heat oven to 375°F. In a large mixing bowl, combine enchilada sauce, salsa, lime, and green chilies. Stir in chicken and season with cumin.

Spoon a thin layer of sauce in bottom of an 8" round casserole (2-quart). If using a square baking dish, simply tear tortillas to fit shape of dish. *Tip:* For an 8" square baking dish, buy small tortillas and trim edges to 4" squares.

Layer tortillas, chicken mixture and cheese, as if making lasagna. Top with a final layer of sauce and cheese. Finish with almonds, if desired.

Bake 35–40 minutes or until bubbly and well heated. Remove from oven and let stand 10 minutes before slicing. Serve topped with a garnish of low-fat sour cream and/or guacamole (see page 10).

> I will not eat oysters. I want my food dead — not sick, not wounded — dead.
>
> — *Woody Allen*
>
> Source: quotegeek.com

Chicken and Bowties in Wine Sauce

Light yet satisfying, this sauce needs to simmer for only 30 minutes to taste wonderful. It's even better when sauce is made in advance and reheated. Serves 3.

In a large saucepan over medium high heat, sauté the onion, garlic, carrot, and celery until soft (4–5 minutes). Season with sea salt and pepper.

Add wine and cook down an additional 2–3 minutes. Stir in the chicken stock, tomato paste, and seasonings. Lower heat and simmer 10 minutes, stirring occasionally.

Add chicken and peas. Continue simmering an additional 10–15 minutes, stirring occasionally.

During the first simmer, bring 4 quarts of salted water to a boil. During the second simmer, cook farfalle (bowties) according to package directions (usually 10–12 minutes) until al dente. Drain then toss with sauce mixture. Serve immediately.

1½ T. extra virgin olive oil

1 medium white or red onion, minced

1 clove garlic, minced

¼ C. carrot, minced (1 large carrot or 7–8 baby carrots)

¼ C. celery, minced (1 stalk)

Sea salt and pepper, to taste

½ C. dry white wine (a little more won't hurt)

1½ C. chicken stock (see page 14)

¼ C. + 1 T. tomato paste

½ t. dried oregano leaves

½ t. dried thyme leaves

1½ C. cooked chicken, bite size

½ C. frozen petite peas

6 oz. farfalle (bow-tie) pasta

Sea salt to taste

> When I was a teenager I got my first job — in a bakery…The more I cooked, the happier people got. Best of all, I was enjoying myself doing it. Now you know why I decided to become a chef.
>
> — Emeril Lagasse
>
> Source: Emeril's *There's a Chef in My Soup!*

Southwestern Chicken and Rice Casserole

Casseroles are great to make ahead and pop in the oven when needed. No need to make side dishes, since everything's in the casserole! Serves 4–5.

---

2 C. cooked long grain rice (1 C. uncooked)

2 T. extra virgin olive oil or butter

2 large cloves garlic, minced

1 C. red onion, diced

1 C. red or green bell pepper, diced

¾ C. zucchini, thinly sliced

1 C. Roma tomatoes, diced

Sprinkle of sea salt, to taste

2 C. cooked chicken (bite size)

¾ C. reduced fat sour cream

1 (4 oz.) can diced green chilies (fire-roasted)

1 C. Mexican cheese blend, shredded (Asiago, Monterey Jack, etc.)

1 T. chopped cilantro, fresh (or 1 t. dried)

Cook rice in a rice cooker or on stovetop, according to package directions.

Meanwhile, in a large skillet over medium heat, pre-heat oil or butter and sauté the garlic, onion, and bell pepper until softened (3–4 minutes). Add zucchini and tomatoes. Sprinkle with salt. Continue to sauté another 4–5 minutes.

Place rice in a 2-quart casserole. Add sautéed vegetables, including liquid. Layer with chicken, sour cream, and green chilies. Top with cheese.

Sprinkle top with cilantro.

Bake at 350°F for 40 minutes, or until hot and bubbly.

Serve hot.

Alektorophobia — Fear of chickens

Chicken Rice Bake Almondine

Dinner for 4 is an easy 20 minutes prep and 20 minutes baking away. If you're in a big hurry, this recipe is very tasty, even without baking. Simply garnish with the cheese.

In a heavy 3-quart saucepan over high heat, combine water, sea salt, and celery. Bring to a boil, add rice and stir. Cover tightly, and reduce heat to maintain a simmer for about 12–15 minutes.

Add peas and pearl onions, and artichokes, but do not stir. Cover and cook an additional 5 minutes or until rice is tender and water is absorbed.

Add chicken and parsley, stir, cover, and set aside until needed.

While rice cooks, melt butter in a 10" skillet over medium heat. Using a wire whisk, stir in flour to make a paste. Gradually add evaporated milk and water, continuing to stir frequently until sauce thickens and comes to a simmer. Combine sauce with the chicken-rice mixture in saucepan.

Serve now with a garnish of cheese, or transfer to a lightly buttered 2-quart baking dish. Sprinkle with cheese and toasted almonds*. Bake at 375°F for 15–20 minutes or until bubbly and lightly browned.

For easier serving, let casserole rest 15 minutes prior to serving.

*For help toasting almonds, see the Recipe Notes on page 12 under "Toasting Nuts."

2 C. water

1 t. sea salt

½ C. celery, diced

1 C. long-grain rice, uncooked

1½ C. frozen petite peas and pearl onions

¾ C. frozen artichoke hearts

1½ C. cooked chicken, diced

2 t. freeze-dried parsley (1 T. fresh)

2 T. butter

2 T. all-purpose flour

¾ C. low-fat evaporated milk

1¼ C. additional water

Sea salt and black pepper

¾ C. shredded cheddar or Monterey Jack cheese

¼ C. toasted slivered almonds (optional)

Somewhat Spicy Chicken Loaf

This chicken loaf is a great place to use up dark meat. Because the chicken is cooked, you can speed things up by starting it in the microwave. For a hearty meal, try open-faced sandwiches on peasant bread with the mushroom gravy and mashed potato recipes on pages 139 and 138. Serves 2.

---

1 ½ C. cooked chicken, diced

¼ C. chicken stock (see page 14)

½ C. white or red onion, minced

¼ C. celery, minced

1 ½ t. freeze-dried parsley, (or ¾ t. dried)

¼ C. milk

1 egg white

Sprinkle of sea salt and ground black pepper

Sprinkle of red pepper flakes

¾ C. soda crackers, finely crumbled

Combine all ingredients in a bowl and mix thoroughly. Add a few drops of additional milk if necessary so that loaf molds together easily. Use your hands to form the loaf and place in a non-metal casserole or loaf pan. Cover with a damp paper towel, and microwave 2 minutes on high (time is for a 1000W microwave).

Transfer loaf to the oven at 350°F, 20 minutes, or until chicken loaf is lightly browned.

To serve, slice loaf and arrange on plate or atop open-faced peasant bread (or other whole grain bread) or mashed potatoes. Serve immediately.

> Once, during Prohibition, I was forced to live for days on nothing but food and water.
>
> — *W.C. Fields*
>
> Source: quotationspage.com

Chicken Cacciatore

The aroma will make you hungry long before this dish is ready. Because the chicken is pre-cooked, it's ready to serve much faster than traditional cacciatore recipes. Don't forget to use the carcass to make chicken stock while the sauce cooks down. Serves 6.

In a 4½-quart saucepan or stockpot, pre-heat olive oil to medium and sauté the onion and garlic cloves 1–2 minutes, until slightly soft. Add mushrooms and sauté an additional 2–3 minutes.

Add stewed tomatoes and tomato paste, increasing heat to bring the mixture to a simmer.

Stir in bell pepper and seasoning to taste. Add chicken, partially cover, and continue to simmer at least 50 minutes, or until sauce cooks down sufficiently and bell peppers are soft.

Cook pasta in salt water according to package directions. Serve cacciatore over pasta with a garnish of Parmesan, and enjoy!

Variation: To get dinner on the table faster, substitute 1 jar (26 oz.) of prepared marinara sauce for two cans of stewed tomatoes. This reduces cooking time to about 30 minutes.

1½ T. olive oil

1 large white or yellow onion, coarsely chopped

3 cloves fresh or freeze-dried garlic, minced

1 C. brown mushrooms, coarsely chopped

3 cans (14 oz. each) diced stewed tomatoes (Italian style)

1 T. tomato paste

2 T. red bell pepper, finely chopped

1 large green bell pepper, cut into thin strips

3 T. fresh or freeze-dried basil, chopped

4 C. cooked chicken

12 oz. pasta (spaghetti, linguini or fettuccini)

½ C. Parmesan cheese, shredded for garnish

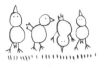

Broccoli and Roast Garlic Chicken Supreme

Few things in life are better than garlic! Here, roasted garlic complements a casserole full of good things, including lots of cheese, chicken (of course) and ham or sausage. Serves 4.

¼ **lb. smoked sausage or ham (we tested Hillshire Farms® "lite" Polish kielbasa and Black Forest turkey ham)**

2 T. butter

2 T. all-purpose flour

½ C. yellow onion, chopped

8 large cloves garlic, peeled but whole

¼ C. white wine

1½ C. whole milk

1½ C. sharp cheddar or cheddar-jack blend cheese

1 t. dried sage

Sea salt and ground black pepper, to taste

2 C. fresh broccoli: bite size pieces par-cooked to 75%

2 C. cooked chicken, bite-size

¼ C. Parmesan to garnish

Chop the sausage into small pieces and brown with 2 T. water over medium heat, about 10 minutes. Set aside until needed. Skip this step if using ham.

Meanwhile, melt butter over medium heat in a deep skillet or chef's pan. Add flour and stir briskly to make a paste. Add onion, garlic cloves, and wine, stirring for another 2–3 minutes. Begin adding milk ½ C. at a time, stirring frequently.

Reduce heat slightly, and stir in cheese and seasonings. Keep stirring until sauce begins to thicken, 3–5 minutes. Add chicken and ham or sausage. Reduce heat to lowest setting. Cover until ready to use.

Pre-heat oven to 375°F.

In a 2-quart baking dish, spread broccoli in an even layer, and add 1 T. water. Cover with a paper towel and microwave on HIGH, 2 minutes or until par-cooked to 75%. When in doubt, it's better to undercook it at this stage.

Cover broccoli evenly with sauce, garnish with Parmesan, and bake uncovered 20 minutes at 375°F. Serve immediately.

Chicken and Tater Tot® Casserole

Inspired by Emeril Lagasse's Man-Oh-Man Potato Casserole recipe in *Emeril's There's a Chef In My Soup*, this recipe is a little lighter, made with chicken rather than ham, cutting back on fat and adding some tasty vegetables that kids won't even notice as they're busy devouring the potatoes and cheese. Serves 4.

Preheat oven to 425°F, with rack in center of oven. Spread tater tots in bottom of an 8" square or other 2-quart baking dish. Bake 15 minutes. Turn potatoes and bake another 10–15 minutes until potatoes begin to crisp. Remove from oven and set aside. Reduce heat to 375°F.

Meanwhile, in a deep 10" skillet, melt butter over medium heat (be careful not to brown butter). Season and sauté onion, peppers and green chilies until soft, 4–5 minutes. When vegetables soften, stir in flour thoroughly. Gradually add the milk plus chicken stock and seasonings. Increase heat to medium-high, stirring often until mixture comes to a boil.

Remove from heat and stir in Monterey Jack cheese and chicken.

Pour the chicken and cheese mixture over the baked tater tots and smooth top. Cover with the cheddar cheese. Bake an additional 25 minutes or until bubbly and lightly browned.

Let casserole rest 5–10 minutes prior to serving. Pair with a fresh-tasting soup or green salad to make a meal!

Variation: Prepare as above, substituting 1 C. chopped Roma tomato and ¾ C. bite-sized asparagus for the red bell pepper and green chilies.

1 package (16 oz.) frozen Tater Tots®

2 T. butter

¾ C. yellow onion, diced

1 C. red bell pepper, diced

¾ C. yellow bell pepper, diced

4 oz. can mild green chilies

¼ t. sea salt

¼ t. black pepper

2 T. all-purpose flour

1 C. milk (2%, whole or soymilk)

¼ C. chicken stock (see page 14; or use "pan drippings" plus water)

1 C. Monterey Jack cheese, shredded

1½ C. cooked chicken, bite size

¾ C. cheddar cheese, shredded

Chizzarole
(Chicken–Pizza–Casserole)

This tasty little casserole features a crust of store-bought biscuits. In the test kitchen, this dish required 20 minutes of prep time, plus 40 minutes to bake. Serves 5–6.

---

2 T. extra virgin olive oil

2 cloves fresh or 1 t. freeze-dried garlic, minced

¾ C. yellow onion, diced

1 C. red bell pepper, diced

1 medium zucchini, sliced or chopped

2 C. brown mushrooms, sliced

Sprinkle of sea salt and black pepper

2 t. fresh or freeze-dried basil

2 C. cooked chicken, bite size chunks

1½ C. pizza cheese, shredded

½ jar (12–13 oz.) prepared marinara sauce

1 package ready-to-bake biscuits (tested with Pillsbury Grands®)

In a large skillet over medium heat, pre-heat oil and sauté garlic, onion and bell pepper, 2–3 minutes. Add zucchini and mushrooms as well as salt, pepper and basil, continuing to sauté 5–7 minutes until juices release and vegetables are soft.

Drain any excess liquid from vegetables and transfer to a 9″ × 13″ baking dish, distributing evenly.

Top vegetables with a layer of chicken followed by the shredded cheese. Continue with a layer of marinara sauce, making sure to completely cover all vegetables and the chicken.

Bake uncovered at 425°, 20 minutes.

While baking, remove biscuits from package and gently tear each in half horizontally (topping a 9″ × 13″ baking dish required 5 biscuits).

Remove chizzarole from oven after 20 minutes and top with biscuits, arranging them so that they are just touching one another (be creative with a pattern if you like).

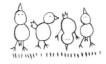

Chizzarole
(Chicken–Pizza–Casserole)

(continued)

Return chizzarole to oven for another 15 minutes, or until deep golden brown. Remove from oven.

Cool 10 minutes. Serve and enjoy!

Variations: Chopped spinach, yellow bell peppers, or just about anything you might put on a pizza (including Canadian bacon) will taste great.

Wine selection: Dishes with chicken in red sauce are always a challenge when choosing wine. Red wines such as Pinot Noir or lighter Merlots make a good choice. Many Chardonnays are bold enough to stand up nicely to red sauce.

A 2001 survey showed that chicken outscored beef and pork on every attribute explored in the survey, which included versatility, taste, ease of preparation, being healthful and nutritious, price, and consistency of quality.

89 percent of Americans ate chicken at least once per week and some 36 percent consumed chicken three times per week or more, according to the survey conducted for the National Chicken Council and US POULTRY by Bruskin Research.

Only 29 percent of respondents consumed chicken once per week, and eleven percent ate chicken less than once each week.

A positive correlation was noted between high chicken consumption and higher household incomes ($50,000 per year or more), as well as college or post-graduate education.

Source: eatchicken.com

Way Down South Jambalaya

Here's a great opportunity to spice things up and serve something very different. Pretend you're in Louisiana and dig in! Despite a fairly long list of ingredients, this recipe withstands a lot of "guesstimating" and goes together quickly. If you need to make it ahead or plan to reheat, reserve the shrimp until ready to serve. Serves 6–8.

1 T. olive oil

¾ lb. smoked sausage (we tested with "lite" Polish kielbasa)

1 C. yellow onion, chopped

½ C. green onions, chopped (white and light green parts only)

2 large stalks celery, chopped

½ C. green bell pepper, chopped

2½ C. chicken stock (see page 14)

12 oz. beer (anything from a lager to an amber ale will do)

½ t. dried rosemary

1 t. dried thyme

1 t. dried parsley

Sea salt

Freshly ground black pepper

Cut the chicken and sausage into small (no larger than bite-sized) pieces.

In a heavy saucepan or Dutch oven over medium heat, brown sausage in the olive oil until done, about 10 minutes (some jambalaya purists insist on lard, but do you really want to eat lard?). Remove the meat from the pan and set aside.

Season the onions, celery and bell pepper with sea salt and pepper, and sauté in pan drippings until tender crisp. If you have more than 2–3 T. of pan drippings, consider discarding the excess to reduce fat content.

Add the chicken stock, beer, seasonings (including additional salt and pepper), and cayenne pepper sauce. Increase heat until the stock starts to bubble, then stir in the sausage and chicken. Add rice and reduce heat to low. Cover and simmer gently for 25 minutes. The rice must remain covered to steam properly. DO NOT STIR during this time.

Way Down South Jambalaya

(continued)

Next, stir in the tomato paste and tomatoes, continuing over low heat for 3–5 minutes. Be sure to stir well with a heavy spoon. If jambalaya seems too dry, add ¼ C. additional stock or water. Taste test for spiciness and adjust if necessary.

If adding shrimp, purchase it pre-cooked or steam or boil it separately in salt water. Add it just prior to serving. Shrimp cooked too long will become rubbery, so monitor carefully to avoid overcooking.

**We tested this recipe with Frank's® Red Hot sauce, but use your favorite or substitute 1–3 T. of cayenne powder. Add cayenne gradually!

Cayenne pepper sauce, to taste (3–8 oz.)**

2 C. cooked chicken (cut to bite size pieces)

2 C. long grain white rice

1 small can tomato paste (6 oz.)

1 C. fresh tomato, chopped

8 oz. cooked shrimp (shelled and deveined)

> Too much food spoils the appetite, and too much talk becomes worthless.
>
> *Chinese proverb*
>
> Source: The Columbia World of Quotations, 1996

Pork & Beans Chicken Casserole

10 minutes of prep time and 45 minutes of baking get you a meal with this easy casserole. The pork & beans just get better as they bake, so serving time can be flexible. Add a dash of cayenne pepper sauce if you're in the mood for spice, and serve over white rice. Serves 4.

---

1 can (15 oz.) pork & beans (testing was done with VanCamp's®)

2 large Roma tomatoes, diced

½ C. plain tomato sauce

1 C. white onion, diced

¼ C. light brown sugar

2 C. cooked chicken

2 t. freeze-dried parsley (1 T. fresh or 1 t. dried)

½ C. shredded sharp cheddar cheese to garnish

Preheat oven to 400°F. In a 2-quart casserole, combine all ingredients except cheese. Stir well, making sure chicken pieces are submerged.

Bake uncovered 20 minutes at 400°F. Reduce heat to 350°F and bake an additional 20–30 minutes. Cover with a glass lid or foil if casserole gets thicker than desired. Serve over white rice with a garnish of cheese.

> Kitchens were different then, too—not only what came out of them, but their smells and sounds. A hot pie cooling smells different from a frozen pie thawing. Oilcloth and linoleum and apples in an open bowl and ruffled rubber aprons make a different aromatic mix from Formica and ceramic tile and mangoes in an acrylic fruit ripener and plastic-coated aprons printed with "Who invited all these tacky people?" And the kitchen sounds. I am not sure that today's kitchen is noisier. But the noises are different. Today you get the song of the food processor and the blender, the intermittent hum of the reefer and the freezer, the buzz-slosh-and-grunt of the dishwasher, the violently audible digestive processes of the waste disposal in the sink. Then it was the whir and clatter of the hand-powered eggbeater, the thunk-thunk-thunk of some-body mashing potatoes, or, in green-pea season, the crisp pop of pea pod and the rattle-rattle-rattle of peas into the pan.
>
> — *Peg Bracken (b. 1918), U.S. humorist*
> *A Window Over the Sink, Harcourt Brace*
>
> Source: bartleby.com/The Columbia World of Quotations. 1996

Side Dishes
and
Sauces

Southwestern-Style Cornbread/Muffins

Several times in this cookbook I've recommended including cornbread with soups and main courses, so I'm sharing my secret recipe for fabulous, fast cornbread and corn muffins. I've been told many times that I make the greatest cornbread, but I have to confess, my "secret recipe" is simply Marie Callender's® cornbread mix with the little twist shown below. I hope you like it! Makes 10–12 muffins or 9 cornbread squares.

---

1 canister Marie Callender's cornbread mix

¼ C. corn meal

½ can (2 of 4 oz.) mild green chilies, diced and drained*

¾ C. white corn, drained (preferably shoepeg corn, if available. Thaw if frozen)

Preheat oven and prepare according to package directions, adding additional ingredients. Add water carefully. You may need slightly less water if green chilies and corn were moist, or slightly more to compensate for corn meal. Batter should be moderately thick.

Too-thin batter will yield better results than too-thick batter which will be dry and crumbly, so when in doubt, add a few drops of liquid.

Bake according to package directions. For muffins, use liners or lightly grease muffin tin with butter or cooking spray. For cornbread, grease an 8" x 8" baking dish.

*If you love green chilies, use the entire can.

▶ *Cooking Tip: Remember, muffins bake much faster, so depending on the size of your pans, begin checking after about 10–12 minutes. When done, muffins should be starting to brown on top and pulling away from the sides of the pan.*

Green Beans with Mushroom Dijon Sauce

Fresh green beans or frozen French cut green beans lend this wholesome dish a hint of sophistication.

In a 10" skillet over medium heat, melt butter and add oil, onion and mushrooms as butter foams. Stir constantly and reduce heat if needed to avoid browning butter. Sauté 4–5 minutes until mushrooms are soft and release their juices.

Meanwhile, begin steaming green beans seasoned with a pinch of salt, 3–7 minutes or until desired crispness. Remove stems from fresh beans prior to steaming.

Sprinkle flour evenly over butter mixture, and stir briskly to incorporate. Stir in chicken stock by small amounts, stirring frequently as it simmers. Add Dijon and white wine, and simmer an additional 2–3 minutes or until desired thickness.

Place green beans in serving bowl and top with mushroom mixture. Serve immediately.

Variation: Kale and Mushrooms. Cook as above except start steaming kale about 10 minutes prior to starting sauce. Kale needs to steam about 20–25 minutes until soft. Be sure to wash kale and trim hard stems before steaming.

1 T. butter

1 T. extra virgin olive oil

¼ C. white onion, minced

1 C. brown mushrooms, sliced

1 T. flour

½ C. chicken stock (see page 14)

2 T. Dijon mustard

2 T. white wine or dry vermouth

1 lb. fresh or frozen green beans, seasoned with salt

Sour Cream & Chive
Mashed Potatoes

Mashed potatoes cooked in chicken stock are a terrific side dish for roast chicken, and the potatoes add wonderful flavor as well as nutrients when stock is reused to make soup. Potatoes do have a high glycemic index (the body turns them to sugar quickly), but they are rich in nutrients, especially when eaten with their skins. I believe it's what you put on them that causes most of the problems, so go easy on the additions and eat moderate portions. Serves 4.

4–5 medium white or red potatoes (or 7–10 smaller new potatoes), cubed with skins

4 C. chicken stock (see page 14)

3 whole green onions (reserve tops for chives)

2 T. low-fat sour cream

½ T. butter

¼ C. chives (minced tops of green onions)

¼ C. milk

Cook potatoes in stock with onions until fork tender. Drain and remove onions (optionally saving stock for soup at a later time).

Cover potatoes and return to medium heat until any remaining liquid evaporates (1–2 minutes). Remove from heat, and add sour cream, butter, chives, and milk. Mash to desired consistency.

Cover tightly until ready to serve (up to 15 minutes without re-heating).

> One cannot think well, love well, sleep well, if one has not dined well.
>
> — *Virginia Woolf*
> *A Room of One's Own, 1929*
>
> Source: quotegeek.com

Mushroom Gravy

Always a favorite, this easy gravy is full of rich flavors that complement your roast chicken perfectly. While similar to the mushroom Dijon sauce for the green beans side dish, this one has the consistency and taste of traditional gravy.

In a 10" skillet over medium-low heat, melt butter and whisk in flour to create a roux. Add drippings from chicken container (swirl additional water in the container or add chicken stock to make at least ½ C.).

Heat slowly, stirring frequently, until simmering. Add onion and mushrooms. Continue to simmer until thickened, about 3 minutes. Stir in milk and then season lightly with salt and pepper. Taste and season, if desired. Use immediately or cover and reduce heat to lowest setting. Pour over individual servings or serve "on the side."

▶ *Cooking Tip: If sauce gets too thick, stir in a small amount of stock or water or a drizzle of white wine.*

1½ T. butter

1½ T. all-purpose flour

½ C. "pan drippings" from chicken container*

1 T. white onion, minced

¾ C. brown mushrooms, sliced

2–3 T. milk (evaporated, 2%, whole or soymilk)

Sea salt, to taste

Ground black pepper, to taste

*See Recipe Notes on page 11 for more information regarding pan drippings.

> Big nations are like chickens. They like to make big noises, but very often it is no more than squabbling.
>
> — *Dr. Albert Schweitzer,*
> Playboy, *December 1963*
>
> Source: quotationspage.com

Tequila Un-Cream Sauce

All the taste of a rich cream sauce without all the fat and calories. Green chilies give this easy sauce a taste of the Southwest. Try it on a vegetable side dish such as steamed green beans and tomatoes as well as on your carved chicken. And don't worry about serving to minors. The alcohol cooks out prior to serving.

1½ T. butter

1½ T. all-purpose flour

½ C. "pan drippings" from chicken container*

2 T. mild green chilies, diced (canned chilies work well here)

2 T. Tequila

Sea salt, to taste

Ground black pepper, to taste

2–3 T. milk (whole or soymilk)

*See Recipe Notes on page 11 for more information regarding pan drippings.

In a 10" skillet over medium-low heat, melt butter and whisk in flour to create a roux. Add drippings from chicken container (substitute or supplement with chicken stock).

Heat slowly, stirring frequently, until simmering. Add green chilies, tequila and seasonings. Continue to simmer until thickened, 3–5 minutes. Add milk and stir to incorporate. Use immediately or cover and reduce heat to lowest setting. Pour over individual servings or serve "on the side" as gravy.

▶ *Cooking Tip: If sauce gets too thick, stir in additional stock or milk. Not too much! A little goes a long way.*

> The average whole chicken sold (fresh) in U.S. supermarkets weighs 3 lbs. 12 oz.
>
> Source: eatchicken.com

Pineapple and Honey
Sauce with Lime

Here's a sweet and sour sauce to jazz up a rotisserie chicken dinner. Steam some rice and a vegetable, and dig in!

In a 10" skillet over medium-low heat, melt butter and whisk in flour to create a paste. Add drippings from chicken container (swirl water in pan to get ½ C. or supplement with chicken stock).

Drain pineapple, reserving 3 tablespoons juice. To saucepan, add reserved pineapple juice, honey, soy sauce, and fresh lime juice. Cook, stirring constantly, until thickened, 3–4 minutes.

Add pineapple to sauce. Increase heat to medium and stir occasionally until well-heated.

Spoon sauce and pineapple over chicken, sprinkling lightly with lime peel, if desired.

Serve alongside or over carved chicken and rice.

1½ T. butter

2 cloves garlic, minced

1 T. all-purpose flour

½ C. "pan drippings" from chicken*

1 20-oz. can pineapple tidbits or chunks in juice

¼ C. honey

2 T. soy sauce

¼ C. fresh lime juice

Sea salt, to taste

Grated lime peel to garnish (optional)

*See Recipe Notes on page 11 for more information regarding pan drippings.

> Sometimes I lifted a chicken that warn't roosting comfortable, and took him along. Pap always said, take a chicken when you get a chance, because if you don't want him yourself you can easy find somebody that does, and a good deed ain't ever forgot. I never see papa when he didn't want the chicken himself, but that is what he used to say, anyway.
>
> — *Mark Twain [Samuel Langhorne Clemens]*
> *The Adventures of Huckleberry Finn, 1885*
>
> Source: The Columbia World of Quotations. 1996.

Balsamic Vinegar and Pinot Noir Sauce

This earthy sauce will add an element of sophistication to a late night supper with a loved one. This sauce is best served with the thigh and leg meat which are stronger in flavor. Steamed asparagus makes a wonderful side dish. Because Pinot Noir is a lighter red wine compared to a Cabernet or Zinfandel, it won't overpower the chicken. Why not light the candles, drink the rest of the wine with dinner and make it extra special? Serves 2.

---

1 ½ T. butter

1 ½ T. all-purpose flour

¼ C. brown mushrooms, sliced

½ C. "pan drippings" from chicken container*

¼ C. Pinot Noir

1 ½ T. balsamic vinegar

2 medium tomatoes (Roma or vine ripened), chopped

Sea salt and ground black pepper, to taste

*See Recipe Notes on page 11 for more information regarding pan drippings.

In a 10" skillet over medium-low heat, melt butter and whisk in flour to create a paste. Add drippings from chicken container (swirl water in pan to get ½ C. or supplement with chicken stock).

Add mushrooms and sauté 4–5 minutes until mushrooms become soft and sauce begins to thicken. Add wine, balsamic vinegar, tomatoes and seasonings. Continue to simmer until desired thickness, 2–3 minutes.

Use immediately or cover and reduce heat to lowest setting. Pour over individual servings or serve "on the side" as gravy.

> Some people ask the secret of our long marriage. We take time to go to a restaurant two times a week. A little candlelight dinner, soft music and dancing. She goes Tuesdays, I go Fridays.
>
> — *Henny Youngman*
>
> Source: quotegeek.com

Pear-Walnut Sauce

In a large skillet over medium heat, melt butter and sauté onion until soft. Reduce heat if needed to avoid browning butter. Sprinkle flour evenly over butter mixture, and whisk to incorporate.

Gradually stir in chicken stock, pear juice, lemon juice and white wine. Gently simmer an additional 5 minutes or until thickened. Add Dijon mustard, diced pear and toasted walnut, cooking 2–3 minutes longer. Sauce should thicken to the consistency of gravy. Add additional stock if necessary to thin.

Serve warm over chicken or "on the side."

2 T. butter

¼ C. white onion, minced

1½ T. flour

½ C. chicken stock (see page 14)

½ C. pear juice (use the juice from canned pears)

2 T. fresh lemon juice

¼ C. white wine

2 t. Dijon mustard

2 canned pear halves, diced

¼ C. toasted walnut halves or pieces (See Recipe Notes on page 12 for toasting instructions.)

> My doctor told me to stop having intimate dinners for four. Unless there are three other people.
>
> — *Orson Welles*
>
> Source: quotegeek.com

The Artful Chicken

Chickens are featured subjects in many if not most artistic styles including cubism, realism, impressionism, Dadaism, and surrealism. Even Pablo Picasso included a number of chickens in his work, as did Francisco de Goya, Marc Chagall, and J.W. Ludlow.

The first known chicken depictions in art date from 3000 B.C. to clay figurines found in the Indus River Valley of present-day Pakistan.

Source: *The Complete Chicken.* Pam Percy. Voyageur Press 2002

"The hen is the wisest of all the animal creations because she never cackles until after the egg is laid."

— *Abraham Lincoln (1809–1865), referring to General Joseph Hooker's overconfidence about beating Confederate forces. Hooker's Army of the Potomac suffered a series of defeats ending at Chancellorsville (May, 1963), after which Hooker was forced to resign his command*

Source: *The Complete Chicken.* Pam Percy. Voyageur Press 2002

Your Chicken Is Cooked

Desserts

My Grandma's Apple Pie

Around the holidays and at birthdays, the requests always roll in for apple pie. The handwritten recipe my Grandma Orcutt taped into my mother's 1950s-vintage Betty Crocker® Cookbook has served me well. I stopped making my own crust years ago reasoning that mine were only better than refrigerated crusts 25% of the time (and another 25% they were worse). Otherwise, it's as my Grandma would have made it. Thanks, Grandma! Serves 8–10.

**1 refrigerated
pie crust, 9-inch**

**4–5 T. butter, divided
(do not substitute)**

½ C. sugar, divided

**9–10 large or
12 small apples**

± ¾ t. ground cinnamon

± ½ t. ground nutmeg

Preheat oven to 400°F. Allow the refrigerated crust to come to room temperature.

Peel, core and slice all but one apple into bite sized pieces no more than ½″ thick. A mix of sweet and tart apples is best. A favorite mix is ¾ Jonathan and ¼ Braeburn, Gala or Golden Delicious. My Grandma preferred Cortland apples.

Place apple slices in a large bowl until ready to use. If apples seem very sweet, sprinkle with 1–2 t. lemon juice.

Unfold and center refrigerated crust on a 9″ glass or ceramic pie plate. Dot half of butter in bottom of crust (dots should be no more than 1 t. each) as well as ¼ C. sugar. If apples seem extra tart, add an additional 2–3 T. sugar.

Pile in the apples. Apples should be heaped several inches above the pie plate. If you can fit the last apple, slice it and add it to the pile.

My Grandma's Apple Pie
(continued)

Top your pie with the remaining ¼ C. sugar and dots of butter. Next sprinkle the cinnamon and nutmeg over the top. It's easiest to sprinkle it directly from the container. Don't worry about measuring; simply sprinkle a light, even layer of cinnamon over the apples, followed by a lighter sprinkle of nutmeg.

Place the top crust on a flat surface and roll it an additional 2" in diameter to accommodate the apples.* Fold the shell in half and use a teaspoon to create vent holes in the crust.

Pick up the folded crust and center it over the pie so that the edges hang evenly over each side when unfolded. Seal the edges, creating attractive flutes by forming the crust between the pinched thumb and forefinger of both hands. Wet your fingers if necessary to aid sealing. If you can see the pie plate through the crust, it's too thin and will burn in the oven. Steal a bit of dough from somewhere you have excess to build up the fluting as needed.

Place the pie on a cookie sheet to catch drippings as the pie bakes. Bake at 400°F for 20 minutes. Reduce temperature to 350°F and continue baking until crust is deep golden brown, about 30–35 additional minutes. If fluting is getting too brown, make a collar of aluminum foil to cover fluted edges.**

Remove pie from oven and cool until ready to serve. Apple pie should rest at least an hour to set filling and facilitate slicing. Serve alone or top with cheddar cheese slices or ice cream. Enjoy, and raise a glass to my Grandma!

*Use a flat drinking glass if you don't have a rolling pin. Start in the center of the unfolded crust and work out to the edges to enlarge the crust diameter by 2".

**To make the foil collar, simply fold a 10" square piece of aluminum foil in half. Tear a semi-circle from the center to form a collar that when unfolded, fits over the fluted edges of the pie.

Chocolate Banana Bread Pudding

Some desserts take all day to make or require precise measurements. Bread pudding requires neither. It's a leftovers dessert that, like the chicken recipes included here, doesn't taste leftover. This is another recipe my Grandma Orcutt made. I've updated it a bit with chocolate and banana, adding flair to an old-fashioned dessert that still deserves plenty of attention. Serves 6–8.

---

4 C. dry French bread (moderately packed)	**1 T. blackstrap molasses**
3½ C. whole milk	**¾ C. sugar**
1 C. bittersweet chocolate	**1 T. vanilla extract**
2 very ripe bananas, thinly sliced	**¼ t. sea salt**
5 eggs, large	**½ C. additional milk**

Preheat oven to 350°F. Tear the bread into 1" pieces (day-old bread is even better than fresh), and combine with milk in a large bowl. Unless bread has a super-hard crust, leave crust on bread.

Using a double boiler (you can make one by putting 2" of water in a medium saucepan and stacking a small saucepan on top), melt chocolate. Cover and set aside to keep warm. Note: Use high quality chocolate. We tested with Ghirardelli® Bittersweet Double Chocolate Baking Chips.

In a medium mixing bowl, use a fork or whisk to combine eggs, molasses, sugar, vanilla, salt, and the additional milk. Fold into bread mixture being careful to distribute evenly. Also fold in chocolate.

Transfer the finished mixture to an ungreased 9" × 13" baking dish. Bake in a water bath (see Cooking Tip below) for 50–55 minutes, or until a knife inserted near the center comes out clean. Loosely cover pan with aluminum foil if it appears to be browning too much before center is fully baked.

Remove from oven and cool slightly prior to serving. Serve warm with a topping of chocolate syrup, whipped cream or vanilla ice cream.

▶ *Cooking Tip: A water bath prevents over-drying or browning at the bottom. To prepare, simply use a larger baking pan than your casserole (it should be about 2" deep) and place approximately 1" of water in the pan. Set the bread pudding dish in center of water bath, and bake as directed.*

3 Heavenly New York Cheesecakes

Sue Grafton is not only a master at writing mystery novels, she also makes Killer Cheesecake. Her "secret" of beating the filling with an electric mixer for 20 minutes made me laugh, because I accidentally discovered the same secret a few years ago. Working on something else in the kitchen, I decided a little extra beating wouldn't hurt the cheesecake. Before I knew it, 15–20 minutes had passed and I had the creamiest and best cheesecake ever. Positively succulent!

Shared recipes between friends are the best recipes. Sue's originated with a long-time friend of her husband's family, Olga Urbach. My recipe came to me from good friend, Jayke Muller, who first found it in Jyl Steinback's, *Recipes for Fat Free Living Desserts Cookbook*. Jayke and I have made some tweaks to Jyl's fat-free recipe, using a combination of non-fat, reduced-fat and regular cream cheese and sometimes adding a topping of fresh fruit.

Try all three, and see which you like best!

Thanks to Sue Grafton and Jyl Steinback for sharing these beautiful desserts, and see the Acknowledgements for more on their websites and writing pursuits.

Recipes below are in their authors' own words with occasional notes added for clarity.

Killer Cheesecake (8")

Let all ingredients come to room temperature.

Crust:

1 inner packet Honeymaid Graham Crackers, crushed in a blender or between two pieces of waxed paper (about 1¼ C.)

¾ stick softened butter (6 T.)

3 T. sugar

Filling:

12 oz. cream cheese

2 eggs, beaten

¾ C. sugar

2 t. vanilla

½ t. lemon juice

Topping:

1 carton sour cream (16 oz.)

5 T. sugar

1½ t. vanilla

Crust: Mix crushed graham cracker crumbs with sugar.

Rub softened butter into the crumbs until evenly distributed and mixture feels like wet cement, holding together when pinched.

Press mixture in the bottom of an 8" springform pan, going a wee bit up the sides if desired.

Bake in a 375°F. oven until lightly browned, 10 minutes.

Filling: Combine and beat until light and frothy, about 15–20 minutes with an electric mixer. Pour into partially baked crust and bake in a 350°F oven for 20 minutes. Allow to cool 5 minutes.

Topping: Blend all ingredients. Carefully pour topping over cake and bake 10 minutes longer. Place in refrigerator for at least 5 hours. Remove from pan and serve.

> Life is uncertain. Eat dessert first.
>
> — *Ernestine Ulmer*
>
> Source: quotationspage.com

No-Fat New York Cheesecake
(9", almost no fat)

Crust: Preheat oven to 350°F.

Combine graham cracker crumbs, sugar, and 2 T. melted margarine in a small bowl. Place mixture into a 9-inch springform pan and press evenly over bottom and 1" up sides.

[Author's note: Jyl's recipe does not require baking the crust.]

Filling: Beat cream cheese and 1¼ C. sugar in a large bowl until well blended. Add the egg substitute, vanilla and lemon juice, and blend until smooth. Pour into springform pan.

Bake in preheated oven for 50 minutes, or until golden brown. Place on wire rack and let stand 15 minutes. Increase oven temperature to 450°F.

Topping: In a small bowl, combine sour cream, sugar and 1 t. vanilla. Mix until smooth. Spoon over top of cheesecake and bake 10 minutes or until topping is set. Refrigerate overnight. Remove from pan when ready to serve.

Crust:

1½ C. Graham Cracker Crumbs, non-fat

¼ C. sugar

2 T. low-fat margarine

Filling:

24 oz. non-fat cream cheese

1¼ C. sugar

1 C. egg substitute

2 t. vanilla

2 t. lemon juice

Topping:

16 oz. non-fat sour cream

¼ C. sugar

1 t. vanilla

> What is food to one, is to others bitter poison.
>
> *— Lucretius*
> *99 BC - 55 BC*
> *De Rerum Natura*
>
> Source: quotationspage.com

Tweaks by Jayke and Lauren
(9", medium fat)

Use Jyl Steinback's recipe, except:

_____

Crust: substitute 3 T. butter for margarine and use regular graham cracker crumbs. Bake the crust 10 minutes at 350°F, and cool at least 10 minutes prior to adding filling.

Filling: Use 8 oz. each of regular, reduced-fat and non-fat cream cheese. We prefer Philadelphia Brand® cream cheese. Be sure to blend filling with an electric mixer on HIGH, 15–20 minutes.

Topping: Use reduced-fat sour cream rather than non-fat. If desired, press fresh raspberries and/or blueberries into the topping before the final bake. Raspberries in a simple heart shape are very romantic for your Valentine!

Refrigerate at least six hours prior to serving.

Whichever version of cheesecake you've made: Enjoy!

> A man may build a complicated piece of mechanism, or pilot a steamboat, but not more than five out of ten know how the apple got into the dumpling.
>
> — *Edward A. Boyden*
> *The Woman's Magazine, April, 1988*
>
> Source: bartleby.com/The Columbia World of Quotations. 1996

Chocolate Coconut Custard

A great meal deserves a great dessert! For me, custard brings back happy childhood memories. OK, my mom never made it, but a local restaurant in my hometown did. This recipe improves that old favorite in the best possible way, by adding chocolate! Most grocers sell Oreo® cookie crusts ready to bake. Serves 6–8.

Preheat oven to 425°F. On a large cookie sheet, place the prepared pie shell beside a single layer of coconut. Bake on center oven rack six minutes or until coconut is golden brown. Monitor carefully to avoid burning. Remove from oven and cool until ready to use.

Meanwhile, in a medium bowl, beat eggs and egg white with a wire whisk or hand mixer until slightly frothy. Add steaming hot water, sweetened condensed milk, vanilla, salt and nutmeg. Blend in remaining coconut, stirring until smooth.

Center baked pie shell on cookie sheet (to improve stability) and fill. Top with toasted coconut. Bake 10 minutes; reduce temperature to 350°F, and bake 25–30 minutes longer or until a toothpick inserted in center of pie comes out clean. Cool to room temperature or refrigerate. Serve!

Refrigerate leftovers.

1 Oreo cookie crust, 9-inch

1¼ C. coconut (½ for toasting, ½ for filling)

3 large eggs plus one additional egg white

1 C. + 2 T. hot water

1 can (14 oz.) sweetened condensed milk

1½ t. vanilla extract

¼ t. sea salt

¼ t. ground nutmeg

Triple Chocolate Cheesecake Muffins

Even if you don't think of yourself as a baker, this is an easy treat that takes less than 25 minutes to prepare and 25 minutes to bake. I like to add flax meal to reduce the need for oil and increase fiber and other good things, but you can also prepare the cake mix as directed on the package. Makes about 24 muffins.

---

1 package dark chocolate cake mix*
¾ C. flax meal
3 eggs
1½ T. canola oil
1½ C. water or milk

Filling:
12 oz. cream cheese, softened
¾ C. sugar
1 t. vanilla extract
1 egg, beaten
6 oz. bittersweet chocolate baking chips

Garnish:
½ C. pecans or slivered almonds (optional)

Preheat oven to 350°F. Prepare muffin pan by adding a paper baking cup to each opening. Set cream cheese out to soften.

Cake: In a large bowl, beat cake mix, flax meal, eggs and water or milk with an electric mixer two minutes or until smooth. If batter seems too thick, add additional water or milk until batter is desired consistency.

Filling: Combine cream cheese, sugar, vanilla and egg. Beat with a fork or electric mixer until smooth. Fold in baking chips.

Muffins: Fill baking cups ¾ with cake batter. Top each muffin with 1 T. cream cheese mixture and one or two pieces of pecan or almonds, if desired.

Bake 25 minutes or until a toothpick inserted in center of muffin comes out clean. Muffins will pull away from the edges of the pan.

Remove from oven and cool for at least 5 minutes prior to serving.

*Tested with Betty Crocker® Super Moist® Cake Mix (dark chocolate), Philadelphia Brand® Cream Cheese and Ghirardelli® Bittersweet Double Chocolate Baking Chips.

▶ *Cooking Tip: to soften refrigerated cream cheese, place the cream cheese in a microwavable container and microwave approximately 30 seconds on 50% power. Monitor carefully.*

Reference

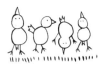

A Chicken in Every Pot

Although chicken is the most broadly consumed meat in the world, raising chickens originally had nothing to do with food. Chickens similar to those raised today were first domesticated in India somewhere between 3200 and 2000 B.C. as fighters, thus creating the first-known spectator sport, cockfighting.

In Western cultures, the Romans were among the first to integrate chicken into their diets as a meat source. As Pam Percy points out in her book, *The Complete Chicken* (Voyageur Press, 2002), it was during the Roman Empire that chicken became a vital part of Europeans' daily diet. Resourceful Romans made numerous advances in the culinary arts, moving away from simply boiling the meat to include spices and marinades. Apicus, a Roman gourmet who lived the first century A.D., is credited with writing the first cookbook of the Western world, one that included the Western world's first chicken recipes.

Chicken worked its way into both lavish feasts and everyday cuisine, at least among the upper classes. Simon Goodenough in *Citizens of Rome* (Random House, 1979) described dinner, generally served in the late afternoon, as the main meal of the day. It might consist simply of vegetables with olive oil for those of the lower class, or an elaborate several-course meal for the well-to-do. Typically, however, dinner consisted of three courses.

• The first course, the "gustus" was the appetizer course consisting of mulsum (wine mixed with honey) along with salads, eggs, shellfish, mushrooms and other appetizers.

• The second course, the meat course, or "lena," might include pork, poultry, fish, game, and/or exotic birds, served with vegetables.

- The final course, called the "secundae mensae," or "second table" was given its name because at dinner parties, the entire table was removed after the first two courses, and a new one put in its place for the final dessert course.

Romans made attempts to fatten and tenderize chickens for more delicious taste, sometimes employing ingenious methods. Practices included dipping live hens in Falernian wine (a heavy, sweet red wine made from Falernian grapes and popular in ancient Rome) and water. Some chefs claimed that tenderizing could be achieved by placing a fig in the chicken's anus.

Every part of the chicken was used in ancient kitchens – the blood, intestines, testicles, rumps, heads, livers, lungs, feet, heads and necks. Crests and wattles were also eaten, in broth or roasted over coals with pepper and orange juice. Chicken brains were a delicacy believed to improve the intellect.

Chicken livers were second in popularity only to those of geese. Romans prized chicken livers roasted on coals as a curative to revive diminishing strength, especially useful when accompanied by a glass of white wine.

Culinary progress accelerated or declined along with the political and economic climate. After a long period of invasions, hardship and famine, gastronomical advances resumed in Europe around the 8th century. With peace, poultry and fish became more plentiful in kitchens and farmers and fishermen were able to distribute a broader variety of goods. The extension of trade to the outer reaches of the known world as well as the impact of the returning Crusaders from exotic locales led to the development of more complex food.

New spices and condiments also necessitated new cooking techniques, and dishes became more elaborate, both in taste and presentation.

In France, feasts and elaborate banquets became the rage among the royalty, and the royal menu often included stuffed capons and other tasty poulets.

But it was during the reign of Henry IV (1553–1610) that chicken became symbolically important. He stated in 1598, "I want there to be no peasant in my kingdom so poor that he is unable to have a chicken in his pot on Sundays." The famous poule au pot was a symbol of modest comfort for all classes. Poule au pot is a stuffed chicken simmered with meat and vegetables, but preparation varies greatly.

Egypt
The ancient Egyptians ate ducks and geese for centuries prior to domesticating chickens imported from India. Thutmos III, a pharaoh of ancient Egypt who ruled from 1504 to 1450 B.C., kept egg-laying birds in his zoo, but actual production of chicken for consumption came much later, probably around 100 B.C. The Egyptians were the first to mass produce chickens and incubate eggs, presumably to feed the throng of pyramid workers. They created the process of incubation in "hatching ovens" and were capable of producing from 15 to 20 million chicks per season.

China
Poultry has been prized in China for nearly 3,000 years. The rooster was believed to possess the yang or cosmic force of the masculine spirit. This appreciation of chicken naturally extended to food. Guided by the standards of Confucius more than 2,500 years ago, chefs integrated the philosophy of harmony, beauty and balance to the preparation and enjoyment of food. Confucius stressed that food should be considered more than life-sustaining. It should come together in perfect harmony with taste, color, texture, aroma and presentation. Chicken was a high point of cuisine, reserved for special occasions. The Chinese introduced hundreds of chicken dishes, giving them poetic names such as "Drunken Chicken" and "Chicken with Golden Pastures."

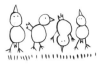

Jewish Influences

Since the early Middle Ages, chickens have been important in Jewish cooking. Farmers could slaughter the chickens themselves, according to kosher laws.

In the Jewish tradition, chicken is standard fare at such social affairs as weddings and bar mitzvahs. The classic Friday night family meal includes chicken soup, followed by roasted or boiled chicken.

A 12th century Jewish physician, Moses Maimonides, is attributed with first suggesting chicken soup as a cure for colds, although chicken soup's curative effect on respiratory ailments is described in Greek texts from as early as 200 B.C.

Scientists now acknowledge that chicken soup (made from fresh or frozen stock and vegetables, not canned broth) does have beneficial medicinal qualities to combat the common cold. Chicken soup reportedly contains compounds that assist in clearing the nasal passages of mucus, thereby inhibiting the spread of viruses and bacteria within the body.

Chicken Comes to North America

Although the native turkey took on a symbolic significance in the early colonies, chickens arrived with the first settlers. The first American cookbook, written in 1796 by Amelia Simmons, included a chicken recipe, and Brunswick Stew (often called "Church Builder Chicken") was a favorite of Thomas Jefferson. From the *Williamsburg Cookbook*:

> "Cut of a three Pound Chicken (or two Squirrels) and put in a large Pan with three Quarts of Water, one large slice Onion, one half Pound of lean Ham cut in small Pieces and simmer gently for two Hours. Add three Pints of Tomatoes, one Pint of Lima Beans, four large Irish Potatoes diced, one Pint grated Corn, one Tablespoon Salt, one fourth Teaspoon Pepper, a small Pod of Red Pepper. Cover and simmer gently for one more Hour stirring frequently to prevent Scorching. Add three ounces of Butter and serve hot."

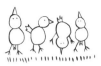

Chicken production as a U.S. industry began in the 1850s in Rhode Island. By this time, the Industrial Revolution was in full swing and limited mechanization reached the poultry industry.

During the 1928 presidential election, the Republican Party, stumping for Herbert Hoover, promised, "a chicken in every pot and a car in every garage." Standards had obviously risen since Henry IV spoke in 16th Century France!

And Finally

Tinker's Chicken

Monica Sheridan, in her book *The Art of Irish Cooking* (1865) described what might be one of the world's most unusual cooking styles in her Tinkers' Chicken recipe. If you're ever stuck on a deserted island with a chicken, it may come in handy.

Generations ago, Tinkers, or Travelers, as they are now known in Ireland, scorned traditional roots and took to the road. They were reputed to enjoy eating any free-range, but foolish, chicken that may have wandered near their caravans. To disguise the bird's misfortune, the Travelers devised an ingenious way of cooking the poor fowl:

1. Wring its neck and kill it
2. Do not pluck or gut the chicken
3. Encase the chicken in a plaster of soft mud
4. Dig a hole one foot deep and place the chicken inside; fill in with dirt and light a fire on top.
5. After three or four hours, when the fire has died down, dig up the chicken
6. Crack the casement, the feathers stick to the clay, and the chicken should be perfectly cooked!

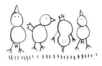

Economical Cooking 101

With just a little planning, one chicken can go a long, long way! It should be routine for you to get six (or more) meals from each chicken purchased. Most of the recipes shown in this book can accommodate (and are enhanced by) a mixture of white and dark meat, so it's really just a matter of making sure the entire chicken is used.

Kept refrigerated, you have about four days from time of purchase to use the chicken. You can extend that by making soup, a baked entrée, or by freezing leftovers.

Here's an example to get you started:

Day 1: Purchase a 2¾–3 lb. chicken for you and your significant other. Serve the leg and thigh portions with Balsamic Vinegar and Pinot Noir Sauce. Enjoy a glass of wine with dinner and relax!

Day 2: The kids and grandkids are visiting (or maybe some friends). Serve *Low-Fat, Extremely Tasty Chicken Lasagna* (serves up to 8 using most of the white meat of your chicken). You'll have time to simmer the carcass in water on the stovetop to make stock while the lasagna bakes, or you can do it later. Add a cup of water at the end to cool, remove bones and skin (leaving any remaining meat) and refrigerate until tomorrow.

Day 3–4: Almost any day is a great day for soup. If you've made the stock, simply skim most of the fat from the top, then proceed to make one of the soup recipes in this book. Southwestern White Bean, Tortellini Chicken Soup, and others such as Tomato Leek Soup can be made with very little chicken meat and will yield 4 6 servings. If you have extra stock, fill an ice cube tray and freeze to flavor sauces, etc.

You get the idea! Rotisserie chickens are an economical and easy way to prepare wonderful yet convenient meals. Don't hesitate to try your own combinations and variations to make cooking fun!

Finding the Best-Tasting Chicken

Here are a few tips summarizing what to look for.

Rotisserie Chicken (purchased pre-cooked at a grocer or warehouse club):
- Look for the largest chickens.
  - When cooking many chickens at the same time, the largest will be closest to ideal in terms of doneness, since all the chickens in a batch will be cooked until the largest are ready.
  - Costco and Sam's Club, two of the major warehouse clubs, each sell around 20 million chickens every year. Minimum cooked weight at both is 2¾ pounds. Costco reports variation up to 3½ pounds.
- Buy the meatiest chicken. Broad-breasted chickens with plump drumsticks will yield the most meat.
- Observe moisture content. Chicken should appear moist and juicy.
- Chicken should be time-stamped or ask someone at the store when it was cooked. If no one seems to know, shop elsewhere.
- Minimally seasoned chickens tend to make the best leftovers and soups.

Whole Raw Chicken (purchased for home rotisseries):
- Skin color should be white or yellow, dependent on the chicken's diet.
- Fresh chickens should be cold to the touch. They may be partially frozen (storage of fresh chicken is between 26°F and 32°F which is cold enough for ice crystals to form) but should not be hard.
- Packaging, if watertight, should contain minimal excess water. Chickens are more than half water, and the more they lose prior to cooking, the less tender the meat will be.
- "Natural," "Minimally Processed," "Kosher," and "Flash Frozen" are all desirable words to see on labels.
- Look for graded poultry. Poultry doesn't have to be graded, but graded poultry will have a more uniform skin, and no broken wings, etc.

Chicken Breeds and Terminology

A descendant of the Southeast Asian red jungle fowl, most chickens raised for meat in America are from one of two breeds: the Cornish (developed in Britain) or the White Rock (developed in New England). Common varieties include:

Broiler-fryer – young chicken about 7 weeks old weighing 2½ to 4½ pounds. Very tender. Most chicken parts sold in U.S. grocery stores are broiler-fryers.

Rock Cornish Game Hen – small broiler-fryers weighing between 1 and 2 pounds.

Roaster – older chicken (3 to 5 months) weighing 5 to 7 pounds. Yielding more meat per pound than a broiler-fryer, roasters are generally roasted whole.

Capon – male chickens, 16 weeks to 8 months old, which are surgically neutered. Weighing 4 to 7 pounds, capons are characterized by large quantities of tender, light meat.

Stewing/Baking Hen – a mature laying hen 10 months to 1½ years old. Less tender meat makes stewing or other moist cooking the best preparation method.

Mini-Glossary

Glossary information comes from the award-winning website, feathersite.com.

- ♦ All chickens, male or female, are properly called chickens. For example, a rooster is also a chicken. They all hatch out as chicks.
- ♦ Young males are cockerels, and become roosters, or cocks, at 1 year of age.
- ♦ Young females are pullets. At 1 year of age they're called hens, unless you're in Australia, then they may be called "chooks" (rhymes with "books"). The term chooks is also applied to all chickens, as in "I've a flock of chooks."
- ♦ Comb -- the fleshy red protuberance on the top of a chicken's head
- ♦ Wattle -- the fleshy red thing hanging under the chicken's beak

What Does the Label Really Mean?

To protect consumers and to provide a means of standardization in the poultry industry, the USDA and other government bodies define a variety of terms used on food labels and regulate the industry accordingly. Here are a few of those terms:

POULTRY is a general term that includes all domesticated birds suitable for food except pigeon and squab. The USDA requires that birds offered for sale in the United States be farm-raised.

FREE RANGE chicken and turkey must have, as the term implies, free access to the outdoors. Reality offers a wide range of environments, from small flocks that wander freely to chickens in small coops with access only to enclosed pens.

The USDA doesn't yet define the term ORGANIC in association with chickens or other poultry, but a definition is pending. USDA currently allows certain poultry to be marked, "Certified Organic by" a third party, and requires certifying bodies to meet certain basic criteria and have standards in place to ensure certified products meet the criteria on an ongoing basis.

Most producers follow the California definition for organic: Birds labeled organic must be raised without antibiotics and their feed must be grown in fields that have been pesticide and chemical-free for at least 3 years.

The term NATURAL is very broadly defined and regulated by the USDA, but in general, it refers to birds which have been minimally processed at the time of sale and contain no artificial ingredients or added color. The term NATURAL doesn't imply anything about what the bird may have been fed or the environment in which it was raised.

KOSHER chickens are processed in accordance with Jewish dietary laws. Rabbis supervise production and perform the ritual slaughtering, after which chickens are cold-water processed and brined (soaked in salt water). The

result is a slightly seasoned chicken that may be of somewhat higher quality than the average supermarket chicken.

HALAL chickens are hand-slaughtered by a person of Islamic faith and handled under Islamic authority in accordance with Islamic law.

Fresh vs. Frozen

FRESH is not as easily defined as one might think. In the world of poultry, the term only means that chicken has not been stored at temperatures below 26°F (the point at which the flesh becomes firm to the touch). But chicken begins to form ice crystals below 32°F, so fresh chicken has usually been at least semi-frozen at some point. When labeled fresh, consumers know that processing occurred recently, because fresh chicken, even held at 26°F, is perishable.

Chickens held at temperatures between 1°F and 25°F are not required to carry any specific labeling, but chickens held at any time during distribution at 0°F or below must be labeled as "frozen" or "previously frozen."

Hormones and Antibiotics

Many people think chickens, especially larger chickens, contain hormones, but that simply isn't true. Use of hormones is strictly prohibited for chickens produced or sold in the United States.

NO ANTIBIOTICS on a poultry label means that sufficient documentation has been provided to the Food Safety Inspection Service (FSIS) that no antibiotics were used in the raising of the poultry. In general, chickens slaughtered in the U.S. must be free of antibiotics at time of slaughter.

Additives

A "food additive" is defined by the Food and Drug Administration (FDA) as "...any substance used to provide a technical effect in foods". The FDA has the responsibility of initial evaluation of additives. Once approved, most day-to-day oversight related to use of additives in poultry is the responsibility of

the Food Safety Inspection Service (part of the USDA). FSIS may apply more strict standards for specific use of additives in poultry or meats. Approval is always conditional, and both the FDA and FSIS have programs to continually review the health status of food additives.

Processed chicken may contain a variety of additives. Of the approximately 2,800 additives used in the United States, by far the most common are salt, sugar and corn syrup. Food additives used in poultry products must be listed on the label in order of greatest use to least (by weight).

When buying pre-cooked chicken, look for rotisserie chickens that contain no MSG, preservatives, artificial flavorings or coloring.

A list of common additives for chicken is shown below with explanations:
- ◆ Water – Chickens are exposed to water during processing, but as a percentage, water added during processing makes a relatively small addition to overall water content. In general, the more lean the meat, the more water.
- ◆ Salt – salt is mainly sodium chloride. Sea salt is sodium chloride from evaporated sea water, plus trace elements such as sulfur, magnesium, zinc, potassium, calcium, and iron. Salt enhances flavor and acts as a preservative.
- ◆ Sodium phosphates are used as an adjustment to bring meat back to normal Ph (acidity) neutral position. At neutral Ph, the meat is best able to retain juices.
- ◆ Modified food starch – (usually cornstarch) Added to help chicken retain moisture.
- ◆ Sugar – sugar in the food industry refers to sucrose, the output of sugar beet and sugarcane production. While more than half of the world sugar supply does come from sugarcane, sucrose is commonly called "cane sugar," even when it is not manufactured from sugarcane.
- ◆ Carrageenan is a powder extracted from various species of red algae. The term carrageenan comes from a coastal town in Southern

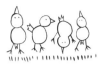

Ireland called "Carragheen" where, many years ago, housewives boiled seaweed (also called Irish moss) to make jellies and puddings. Today, carrageenan is used in low-fat products primarily to help give them the "mouth feel" many consumers expect. Carrageenan also contributes to moisture retention.

♦ Lecithin is a soy extract that works as an emulsifier helping dry particles react with water and avoid clumping. Used to improve product consistency.

♦ Chicken Flavor may contain yeast extract, additional salt, maltodextrin and milk products including dried whey, egg yolk and milk powder.

♦ Flavorings may be spices or spice extractives. Because spices impact flavor rather than nutrient content, regulators don't require them to be separately identified.

♦ Yeast Extract – First produced in 1903, yeast extract is a derivative of brewer's yeast. Once an unwanted byproduct of beer production, it is now a valuable vegetarian food source. More popular in the U.K. than in the U.S., yeast extract is high in B vitamins including B12, folic acid, riboflavin, and niacin. During both World Wars, Marmite®, the original yeast extract brand, was served to soldiers and was considered a valuable food supplement for POWs.

♦ Xanthan gum – Developed by the USDA, xanthan gum is a derivative of dextrose (corn sugar) similar in function to carrageenan.

Water

Uncooked chicken is approximately 68% water, and cooked chickens (broiler-fryers) average 60% water. As a comparison, human males (uncooked, of course) contain an average of 60% water.

In chickens, most water occurs naturally in the muscles. Retention of this water is important for good flavor. During processing, chicken may gain no more than 8% water if under 4½ pounds, and no more than 6% if greater than 4½ pounds.

Freezing causes water in the muscles to expand, damaging the cell walls. When chicken is "flash frozen," chilling occurs very quickly and smaller ice crystals form. These smaller crystals are less damaging to the cell walls of the chicken, allowing it to retain more moisture as it thaws, and resulting in a higher quality product.

Refrigerated raw chicken loses water the longer it remains refrigerated (or when it has been repeatedly frozen and thawed), so choose chicken packages with little visible water.

Safe Handling

Fully-cooked rotisserie (or fast food chicken) should be hot at time of purchase. If you purchase chicken from a reputable store that sells in high volume, that shouldn't be an issue. When in doubt, ask. If the chicken has been on the warmer table too long (more than two hours), chances are that aside from safety issues, it's overcooked and the meat is dry.

Be careful how you handle the chicken between the time of purchase and serving time. Don't leave chickens in a warm car, for example.

Pre-cooked rotisserie chicken should be used within two hours or refrigerated promptly. The USDA recommends cutting the chicken into pieces and storing in shallow, covered containers. Whole chickens may also be stored in their original containers. If you've placed them in plastic bags for the trip home, remove the bags or makes sure they're fully open to allow faster cooling. I've noticed that the addition of a single plastic bag can slow cooling dramatically.

Bacteria can grow on meats when they are at temperatures between 40°F–140°F, so be careful to minimize the time your chicken spends in this range.

Purchase rotisserie chicken as well as fresh meats last before leaving the store. It's smart to place both fresh and cooked meats in disposable plastic

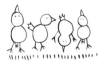

bags to contain any leakage and eliminate cross-contamination between raw and cooked foods or produce.

Keep fresh meats separate from rotisserie chickens in your food basket and vehicle. Rotisserie chickens are too hot to be cooled effectively without proper refrigeration (below 40°F). Most thermal containers won't extend the time you have (2 hours from completion of cooking) to get cooked chicken into refrigeration since bacteria multiply rapidly between 40°–140°F). Eat immediately upon arriving home, or refrigerate promptly then reheat in the microwave or oven to at least 165°F.

At home, immediately place chicken in a refrigerator that maintains 40°F or below, and use within 3 or 4 days, or freeze at 0°F. Remember, contamination from improper handling causes most food borne illness, so practice safe handling techniques for cooked chicken similar to those you use for raw chicken:
- Keep cooked and raw foods separate to prevent cross contamination (use bags as noted previously).
- Wash hands, utensils and cutting boards thoroughly after contact with cooked chicken. For example, don't use a knife to cut cooked chicken then make salad with the same, unwashed knife.
- Bring sauces made with "pan drippings" to a full boil prior to serving.

A Few Facts About Uncooked Chicken:
- Fresh (uncooked) chicken should always feel very cold to the touch when purchased.
- Washing raw chicken is unnecessary, according to the USDA, because bacteria that might be present are destroyed by cooking. [Author's Note: I wash all raw chicken and plan to keep doing so.]
- Although many people think the pink liquid in packaged fresh chicken is blood, it is actually mostly water absorbed by the chicken during chilling and released from the cell walls. Only a small amount of blood remains in the muscle tissue of chicken after slaughter.
- "[Government] inspection of chicken is mandatory but grading is voluntary. Chickens are graded according to USDA Agricultural

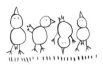

Marketing Service regulations and standards for meatiness, appearance and freedom from defects. Grade A chickens have plump, meaty bodies and clean skin, free of bruises, broken bones, feathers, cuts and discoloration." U.S. Department of Agriculture web site: http://www.fsis.usda.gov

- Whole (uncooked) chickens may be stuffed, but do so immediately prior to roasting. The USDA's Food Safety Inspection Service Hotline recommends that consumers don't pre-stuff whole chicken to cook at a later time or purchase pre-stuffed raw chicken products. Stuffed frozen chicken products should be cooked in the oven from frozen.
- Refrigerated raw chicken may be marinated up to 2 days. Always discard leftover marinade.

How Long Does it Keep?

Cooked chicken should be eaten within 3 to 4 days for best taste, and may be served cold or reheated. Can't remember how long it's been in there? Let your nose and eyes be your guide. When spoilage bacteria form, chicken begins to look and feel slimy, and it no longer smells fresh. Fortunately, spoilage bacteria don't make people sick, and any bacteria present will be killed with cooking.

Bottom line, if a refrigerated chicken looks and smells fine, it is fine. Use it in casseroles or soups that will be brought to temperatures above 165°F, and serve it with confidence. Once you've re-cooked the chicken, you again have 3–4 days to use it if properly refrigerated.

If chicken appears spoiled, don't eat it. No amount of cooking will bring back the taste. Also, the discussion above applies only to cooked foods that have been properly refrigerated.

Chicken you won't use within four days should be frozen. While it's safe to freeze whole cooked chickens, for convenience you may prefer to cut them into single servings. For best quality, flavor and texture, freeze chicken in tightly sealed freezer containers or bags, and use within 4 months.

USDA Recommendation For:	Refrigerator Storage Times
Cooked Chicken, Leftover	3 to 4 days
Chicken Stock or Gravy	1 to 2 days
Cooked Chicken Casseroles, Dishes or Soup	3 to 4 days
Cooked Chicken Pieces. covered with broth or gravy	1 to 2 days
Take-Out Convenience Chicken (Rotisserie, Fried)	3 to 4 days
Chicken Salad	3 to 5 days

Source: USDA

For more information, visit www.fsis.usda.gov or call the USDA Meat & Poultry Hotline at 1.800.535.4555. Thanks to Bessie Berry, manager of the Hotline, and her staff for their kind assistance.

Cooking Your Own

Chicken products come in a multitude of forms today: boneless, skinless, whole, quarters, individual pieces, etc. For home cooking, boneless, skinless chicken breasts are the most popular form of chicken sold in the U.S., according to the National Chicken Council.

Millions of people now own home rotisseries, and this can be a convenient, healthy, and economical way to prepare whole chicken as well as other foods.

In terms of value, whole chicken is often a fraction of the cost of boneless, skinless breasts. Whole chicken has more waste, but shoppers generally pay a premium for chicken breast meat, based on demand.

From a nutritional perspective, both drumsticks and thighs do have more total fat than breast meat, but the difference in saturated fat (the type you most want to avoid) is negligible. See the table at the end of this section for more details.

Skin on, skin off: In general, you'll get the best results (with no difference in fat and calories) cooking chicken pieces with the skin on to help retain moisture. However, as Jacques Pepin points out in *Julia and Jacques: Cooking at Home*, it may be advisable to remove the skin when cooking with a lot of moisture to reduce the amount of fat rendered into the pan (if you'll be making sauce). In moist cooking, the skin doesn't get crispy, it only gets mushy.

Roasting a whole chicken: Perfectly roasted chicken is an attainable goal, but everyone you ask will suggest a different method. Although I have prepared whole chickens in a home rotisserie as well as smoking and frying them, I haven't roasted a chicken since discovering the rotisserie chicken section of my local food warehouse a few years ago. Everyone should know how, though, and here's an easy method.

Start with a well-cleaned chicken, patted dry and liberally salted with legs trussed (bound just tightly enough to keep them in place). Place seasonings in the cavity if desired. Lemon slices (which you should squeeze), onion, garlic, thyme, and rosemary are all good choices.

Start the chicken at 425°F for 20 minutes (25–30 if over 3½ pounds).

If the breast doesn't appear particularly plump, many experts suggest roasting the chicken on its side, putting a few drops of olive oil in the pan to prevent sticking and turning the chicken mid-way through the cooking time.

Basting: You'll find different recommendations from every chef you ask, but if you baste, a good idea from Jacques Pépin is to either remove the chicken from the oven completely or do it very quickly to maintain proper cooking temperature. I like to baste once during the last 15–20 minutes of roasting. Jacques Pépin says he, "almost never bastes."

If at the basting point, the chicken hasn't browned evenly, consider placing the chicken breast-side-up again so that both sides are browned. Looks are only important when bringing the bird to the table for carving, so this is optional.

See the table on the next page for cooking times. When you think it's done, remove from the oven and test first to see that the legs move easily in the hip sockets. If so, continue to test for doneness by inserting a meat thermometer.

Although several reference sources direct chefs to observe the color of the juices to assess doneness, those texts are outdated. USDA does not consider color to be an accurate measure of doneness. An instant-read thermometer should read at least 160°F in the breast and 170°F in the leg and thigh.

If your chicken isn't yet done, stop piercing it! Return the chicken to the oven and wait at least an additional 10 minutes before testing again. If the exterior is getting too brown, cover loosely with aluminum foil.

When done, let the chicken rest at least 15 minutes prior to carving.

Here's what master chef Jacques Pépin has to say about chicken quality and whether to baste, or not to baste:

> …even regular supermarket chickens in the United States are on the whole excellent buys for the price, and although people often say that chickens don't taste as good as they used to, I believe ordinary supermarket chickens are better today. Thanks to improvements from cross-breeding, the meat is more moist and tender than it has ever been. When I was a teenage apprentice, the chicken had to be constantly basted and rested upside down after roasting in order to keep the breast moist, but today it is almost impossible to dry out the breast.
>
> – *Jacques Pépin*
>
> *Source:* Julia and Jacques Cooking at Home
> *Julia Child and Jacques Pépin*
> *Alfred A. Knopf, 2000*

The USDA publishes the cooking guidelines below to help you when cooking chicken parts or whole chicken. Reheated chicken should be brought to 165°F.

Chicken Part	Internal Temperature	Approximate Roasting Time (350°F)
Leg quarters, bone in, 4–8 oz.	170°F	40–50 minutes
Thigh, bone in, 5–7 oz.	170°F	30–40 minutes
Thigh, boneless, 3 oz.	160°F	20–30 minutes
Breast, bone in, 6–8 oz.	170°F	30–40 minutes
Breast, boneless, 4 oz.	160°F	20–30 minutes
Whole chicken	180°F*	
3–5 lb. (broiler)		1¼–1½ hours
6–8 lb. (roaster)		1½–2¼ hours
Ground chicken, 6 oz. patty	165°F	20–30 minutes

Source: USDA

*Author's Note: These are the USDA recommendations, but in my opinion, only the dark meat can withstand such high temperature. My research as well as personal experience suggests a temperature of 170°F (measured in the thigh) is preferable.

Nutrition Facts

Chicken is a great choice for people who want to maintain a healthful lifestyle. Low in calories and saturated fat compared to other meats, rotisserie chicken is an especially good choice, because no added fats are required in cooking.

Recipes included in this book minimize added fat, and where possible, try to use oils high in monounsaturated fats, such as olive oil and macadamia nut oil.

For both economy and good health, feel free to reconsider that drumstick and indulge (but take the skin off prior to eating)!

The thigh and wing portions of the chicken are highest in fat, including saturated fat. Leaving the skin on adds an estimated 5–7 grams of fat and perhaps more if the chicken was marinated or basted. Skinless 3 oz. portions of breast, wing, thigh, and leg meat compare as follows, according to the USDA:

	Calories	Protein (gm)	Total Fat (gm)	Saturated Fat Fat (gm)	Cholesterol (mg)
Breast	120	24	2	1	70
Wing	150	23	6	2	no data
Thigh	150	21	7	2	no data
Drumstick	130	23	4	1	80

Source: Nutri-Facts Fresh Labeling Program, 1995 and USDA Nutrient Database for Standard Reference, Release 11–1, 1997.

Interestingly, it makes no difference from a fat and calories standpoint if skin is removed before or after cooking. From a taste perspective it makes a big difference. As mentioned earlier, leave skin on when cooking or reheating to preserve moisture, but remove it prior to eating.

Wine with Chicken Guide

The most important thing to remember about choosing the right wine for a meal is to follow your own taste buds and preferences. That said, certain food-wine combinations do taste better than others, and some foods such as asparagus, artichokes, avocadoes and salsa/chili peppers have a reputation of being very difficult to match. (By the way, with asparagus and artichokes, I like Chardonnay. With spicy salsa, I opt for beer).

Since white wine is more acidic, it should be served chilled to about 50°F. Store a bottle you'll be drinking soon in the refrigerator and remove it 10–15 minutes prior to serving. Red wines (more tannic) are served warmer, but not room temperature. Serve red wine between 60°F–65°F. Try refrigerating it for 15–20 minutes prior to serving.

When serving wine at home, unless you're having a large party, you'll probably have one wine for the entire meal, so take a "total meal" view of your wine selection. A good first step is to assess the heaviness of your meal.

Chicken is lighter than beef, so most people automatically think white wine when they think chicken. But keep thinking. Many sauces, spices, and side dishes can pull chicken into a realm that merits a red. If you happen to prefer red wines, that's all the more reason to think red with chicken and choose your recipe accordingly.

Which wines are most heavy? Which are lightest? See the table on page 178 for relative weights. When in doubt, consider sparkling wine, an all-around choice that can complement almost any dish.

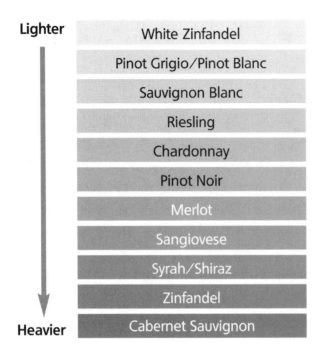

Lighter

White Zinfandel

Pinot Grigio/Pinot Blanc

Sauvignon Blanc

Riesling

Chardonnay

Pinot Noir

Merlot

Sangiovese

Syrah/Shiraz

Zinfandel

Cabernet Sauvignon

Heavier

The End

There you have it! I hope you've found the reference material helpful. I also hope you try and enjoy these recipes for many years to come. Feel free to provide feedback at:

chicken@fallbrookpress.com

Index

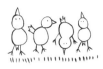

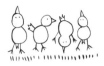

Quotations Index

Order Form – *Your Chicken Is Cooked*

Almost everyone eats chicken! This book makes a great gift or fund-raiser. Contact us to discuss quantity discounts and customization.

Ordering Options:

• Send a copy of this order form with your check payable to Fallbrook Press or your credit card number. Please verify our address online or by phone prior to mailing.

• Visit *www.YourChickenisCooked.com* to order securely via the Internet using your credit card.

• *Contact the publisher to place an order or to discuss how we can meet your special needs.*

By e-mail: chicken@fallbrookpress.com
By phone: Toll-free (888)432-9984 (Call anytime!)

Price: $16.95 each

Shipping & Handling Charges:
USPS Priority Mail or Standard Ground: $4 for 1st book;
Free shipping via USPS Priority mail (or similar)
when 2 or more books ship to the same address

Tax: California shipments add $1.31/book sales tax

Name:_____

Telephone: (   )_____Day / Evening

Payment: ☐ Check Enclosed
           ☐ Please charge my: ☐ VISA ☐ MasterCard
           Cardholder Signature: _____
           Card # _____
           Expiration Date: _____

Shipping Address:_____

City/State/Province _____ Zip _____

☐ **Please autograph my book(s)! (Author signature on title page)**

Return Policy:
We want you to be completely satisfied with your purchase.
Please contact us if you wish to return an item.

Order Form – *Your Chicken Is Cooked*

Almost everyone eats chicken! This book makes a great gift or fund-raiser. Contact us to discuss quantity discounts and customization.

Ordering Options:

• Send a copy of this order form with your check payable to Fallbrook Press or your credit card number. Please verify our address online or by phone prior to mailing.

• Visit *www.YourChickenisCooked.com* to order securely via the Internet using your credit card.

• *Contact the publisher to place an order or to discuss how we can meet your special needs.*

By e-mail: chicken@fallbrookpress.com
By phone: Toll-free (888)432-9984 (Call anytime!)

Price: $16.95 each

Shipping & Handling Charges:
USPS Priority Mail or Standard Ground: $4 for 1st book;
Free shipping via USPS Priority mail (or similar)
when 2 or more books ship to the same address

Tax: California shipments add $1.31/book sales tax

Name:_____

Telephone: (   )_____Day / Evening

Payment: ☐ Check Enclosed
       ☐ Please charge my: ☐ VISA ☐ MasterCard
       Cardholder Signature: _____
       Card # _____
       Expiration Date: _____

Shipping Address:_____

City/State/Province _____Zip _____

☐ **Please autograph my book(s)! (Author signature on title page)**

Return Policy:
We want you to be completely satisfied with your purchase.
Please contact us if you wish to return an item.